Advancing with AutoCAD R13 for Windows

Other titles from Bob McFarlane

Beginning AutoCAD   ISBN 0 340 58571 4

Progressing with AutoCAD   ISBN 0 340 60173 6

Introducing 3D AutoCAD   ISBN 0 340 61456 0

Solid Modelling with AutoCAD   ISBN 0 340 63204 6

Starting with AutoCAD LT   ISBN 0 340 62543 0

Advancing with AutoCAD LT   ISBN 0 340 64579 2

3D Draughting using AutoCAD   ISBN 0 340 67782 1

Beginning AutoCAD R13 for Windows   ISBN 0 340 64572 5

Modelling with AutoCAD R13 for Windows   ISBN 0 340 69251 0

Advancing with AutoCAD
R13 for Windows

Robert McFarlane
MSc, BSc, ARCST, CEng, MIMech E, MIEE, MILog, MIED

*Senior Lecturer, Department of Integrated Engineering,
Motherwell College*

A member of the Hodder Headline Group
LONDON • SYDNEY • AUCKLAND

Copublished in North, Central and South America by
John Wiley & Sons Inc., New York • Toronto

To Linda McFarlane RN and Stephen McFarlane RMN.
Good luck in you new careers.

Also to Helen.
Enjoy your deserved retirement.

First published in Great Britain 1997 by Arnold,
a member of the Hodder Headline Group,
338 Euston Road, London NW1 3BH

Copublished in North, Central and South America by
John Wiley & Sons Inc., 605 Third Avenue,
New York, NY 10158-0012

British Library Cataloguing in Publication Data
A catalogue record for this book is available from the British Library

Library of Congress Cataloging-in-Publication Data
A catalog record for this book is available from the Library of Congress

ISBN 0 340 69187 5
ISBN 0 470 23752 X (Wiley)

Produced by Gray Publishing, Tunbridge Wells, Kent
Printed and bound in Great Britain by The Bath Press, Bath
and The Edinburgh Press Ltd, Edinburgh

Contents

Preface

This book is intended for the more experienced AutoCAD R13 user. The reader is assumed to be familiar with the basic R13 commands and can draw in two dimensions and add hatching, dimensions, text styles, etc. The ability to use icons and dialogue boxes is essential. Readers not familiar with these concepts are advised to obtain *Beginning AutoCAD R13 for Windows* also published by Arnold.

The aim of this book is to introduce the user to the more 'advanced' topics contained within AutoCAD R13, i.e. attributes, customization of linetype, hatch patterns, menus and slide shows. After working through the exercises in the book, readers will be proficient AutoCAD R13 users and their productivity rate will have increased dramatically.

This book will provide an ideal companion to my two other AutoCAD R13 books, and will provide excellent background for any AutoCAD R13 user. The topics in the book will provide a sound grounding for several of the City & Guilds CAD schemes as well as for students studying the SCOTVEC Higher National Certificate (HNC) and Higher National Diploma (HND) courses in Computer Aided Draughting and Design (CADD) which the author pioneered and developed at Motherwell College.

Using the book

The book is an interactive teaching aid, i.e. the user will learn by completing worked examples. The various different command entry methods will be described as will the AutoCAD prompts. Dialogue boxes will be displayed when considered relevant to the topic being discussed.

The following format has been adopted:

1 AutoCAD R13 prompts will be in typewriter face.

2 User responses will be in **BOLD** type.

3 The symbol <R> or <RETURN> will require the user to press the return/enter key.

4 New icons will be displayed when appropriate.

5 A two-button mouse has been assumed and the terms:

   a) pick: requires a left-click

   b) right-click is obvious.

Saving completed work

Most CAD users store their drawings in a directory, and this practice should be continued. For convenience, I will use a directory called **R13CUST** and this directory name will be referred to continually throughout the book.

Standard sheet

AutoCAD users will have their own standard sheet, i.e. prototype drawing. In this book, all work will be completed on A3 sized paper unless otherwise stated. The following are my recommendations for a standard sheet:

a) BLIPS: OFF
b) SNAP: **5**; GRID: **10**
c) UNITS: decimal to 2DP; decimal angles to 0DP
d) All linetypes loaded with LTSCALE and set to 12
e) LIMITS: 0,0 to 420,297
    drawing area: a rectangle from 0,0 to 380,270 on layer 0
f) LAYERS: 0   white   continuous   general use

OUT	red	continuous	outlines
CL	green	center	centre lines
HID	yellow	hidden	hidden detail
DIM	magenta	continuous	dimensions
TEXT	blue	continuous	text items
SECT	cyan	continuous	hatching

    Other layers may be added as appropriate
    Layer OUT should be current
g) Toolbars: Draw, Modify, Object Snap displayed
    Other toolbars will be displayed when required
h) Grips: 0 PICKFIRST: 0
i) Text style: name – **STDA3**
    text font – romans.shx
j) Dimension style: name – **STDA3**

Geometry –	spacing:	**10**
	extension:	**2.5**
	origin offset:	**2.5**
	arrowheads:	closed filled; size: **3**
	centre:	mark; size: **2**
Format –	user defined	
	fit:	text and arrows
	horiz just:	centered
	text:	inside horiz off
		outside horiz on
	vertical just:	above
Annotation –	text: style:	**STDA3**
	height:	**3**
	gap:	**1.5**
	round off:	0

k) Standard sheet name **STDA3** in **R13CUST** directory.

Chapter 1

Attributes

Attributes allow text information to be added to blocks. This information could include details about cost, size, part numbers, material, etc. Attribute data can be extracted from the drawing and used as input to other software packages, e.g. databases, CNC systems, etc. We will demonstrate how attributes are created with a worked example.

Basic information

A computer shop has in its window six different makes of computer, each displaying a different software package. For easy reference, the shop owner has a drawing of the window layout and each computer is represented on the drawing by an icon containing information about the position in the window, the computer make, RAM size, cost and the software being displayed. This drawing information is given in Fig. 1.1(a), and it is this data which is to be added as attributes.

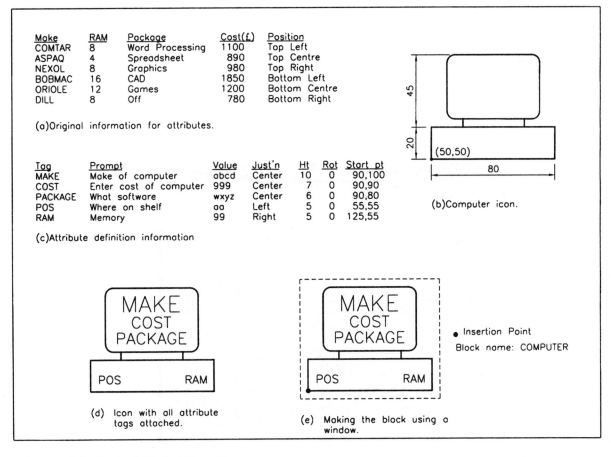

Make	RAM	Package	Cost(£)	Position
COMTAR	8	Word Processing	1100	Top Left
ASPAQ	4	Spreadsheet	890	Top Centre
NEXOL	8	Graphics	980	Top Right
BOBMAC	16	CAD	1850	Bottom Left
ORIOLE	12	Games	1200	Bottom Centre
DILL	8	Off	780	Bottom Right

(a) Original information for attributes.

Tag	Prompt	Value	Just'n	Ht	Rot	Start pt
MAKE	Make of computer	abcd	Center	10	0	90,100
COST	Enter cost of computer	999	Center	7	0	90,90
PACKAGE	What software	wxyz	Center	6	0	90,80
POS	Where on shelf	aa	Left	5	0	55,55
RAM	Memory	99	Right	5	0	125,55

(c) Attribute definition information

(b) Computer icon.

(d) Icon with all attribute tags attached.

(e) Making the block using a window.

Insertion Point
Block name: COMPUTER

Figure 1.1 Basic attribute information.

Making the icon

Before attributes can be defined, it is usual to have some reference drawing to which they can be 'attached'. As our example involves a computer shop window, our reference drawing will be a computer icon, so:

1   Start AutoCAD R13 and open your STDA3 standard sheet from the R13CUST directory. Layer OUT current.

2   Refer to Fig. 1.1(b) and draw the computer icon to the sizes given.

Use your discretion for sizes which are not specified. The only requirement is to have the lower left corner of the icon at the point 50,50 to assist with positioning the attributes.

3   Make layer TEXT (blue) current.

4   Display the Attributes toolbar.

Defining the attributes

Refer to Fig. 1.1(c) which gives details about all the attributes to be added and:

1   From the menu bar select **Construct–Attribute...**
   prompt   Attribute Definition dialogue box
   respond   a) enter **MAKE** in Tag box
         b) pick Prompt box and enter **Make of computer**
         c) pick Value box and enter **abcd**
         d) alter Justification to **Center**
         e) ensure **STDA3** is the Text Style
         f) alter Height to **10**
         g) ensure Rotation is **0**
         h) alter Insertion Point to X: 90
                        Y: 100
                        Z: 0
         i) dialogue box should resemble Fig. 1.2
         j) pick OK.

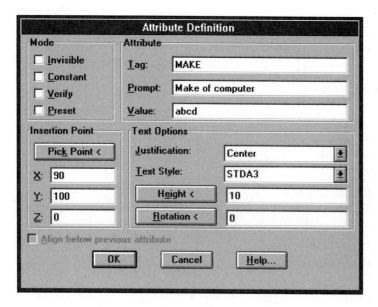

Figure 1.2   Attribute definition dialogue box.

2 The attribute tag **MAKE** will be displayed in the computer icon, centred on the point 90,100.

3 At the command line enter **ATTDEF** <R> and:

prompt	`Invisible: N Constant: N...`
respond	right-click
prompt	`Attribute tag` and enter **COST** <R>
prompt	`Attribute prompt` and enter **Enter cost of computer** <R>
prompt	`Default attribute value` and enter **999** <R>
prompt	`Justify/Style...`
enter	**C** <R> – centre text option
prompt	`Center point` and enter **90,90** <R>
prompt	`Height` and enter **7** <R>
prompt	`Rotation angle` and enter **0** <R>

4 The attribute tag **COST** will be displayed in the icon.

5 The details for the other three attributes (PACKAGE, POS, RAM) have still to be added to the icon. The attribute definition command can be activated:

a) from the menu bar with Construct–Attribute
b) by entering ATTDEF at the command line
c) by selecting the Define Attribute icon from the Attribute toolbar.

6 Using any (or all) of the three methods, add the remaining attributes to the computer icon using the information in Fig. 1.1(c).

7 When the five attributes have been defined, the computer icon will be displayed with the tags positioned as Fig. 1.1(d).

Making the block

When all attributes have been defined, the computer icon symbol and the tags have to be made into a block, so:

1 From the menu bar select **Construct**
                    Block

prompt	`Block name (or ?)`
enter	**COMPUTER** <R>
prompt	`Insertion base point`
enter	**50,50** <R> (or pick the point)
prompt	`Select objects`
respond	**window the icon and tags** then right-click as Fig. 1.1(e).

2 The icon disappears.

3 Remember OOPS?

Attribute nomenclature

When attributes are being defined there are three words which are continually used, these being tag; prompt and value.

Tag: this is the name (or label) given to the attribute. Tag names are usually meaningful and it is the tag which is displayed. Tag names should not have spaces, e.g.

           MY_NAME is permissible
           MY NAME is not permitted

Prompt: this should be a word or phrase which conveys a message to the user (which may not be you). When the block is being inserted, the prompt will be displayed at the command line or in a dialogue box.

Value: this is a default for the attribute and is displayed in < > brackets after the prompt. I generally use abcd or 999, but any alphanumeric entry is permissible.

Inserting the block with attributes

There are two methods for inserting a block containing attributes, the method being controlled by the ATTDIA (attribute dialogue) system variable and:

ATTDIA: 0 – keyboard entry method
ATTDIA: 1 – dialogue box entry.

1 At the command line enter **ATTDIA** <R> and:
 prompt New value for ATTDIA<?>
 enter **0** <R>

2 Refer to Fig. 1.3

3 From the menu bar select **Draw**
        Insert
        Block...
 prompt Insert dialogue box
     ensure X at Specify Parameters on Screen
 then left-click on Block...
 prompt Defined Blocks (in current drawing) dialogue box
 respond pick COMPUTER then OK
 prompt Insert dialogue box
     with COMPUTER as Block name
 respond pick OK
 prompt ghost image of icon
     and Insertion point
 enter **20,180** <R>
 prompt X scale... and enter **1** <R>
 prompt Y scale... and enter **1** <R>
 prompt Rotation... and enter **0** <R>
 prompt Enter attribute values
     What software?<wxyz>
 enter **Word Processing** <R>
 prompt Enter cost of computer<999>
 enter **£1100** <R>
 prompt Make of computer?<abcd>

enter	**COMTAR** <R>
prompt	`Position<aa>`
enter	**Top Left** <R>
prompt	`Memory<99>`
enter	**8** <R>

4 The computer icon will be positioned at the insertion point and will display the attribute information added – fig. (a).

5 *Note.*

    a) the order of your attribute prompts may differ from mine but you should still be able to enter the correct information

    b) the Specify Parameters on the Screen option with the Insert dialogue box is a toggle effect and:

        ON (X in box): insertion point entered from keyboard

        OFF (no X): insertion point entered using dialogue box.

    c) the Insert dialogue box has two block options:

        Block: for blocks created in current drawing

        File: for wblocks (other drawings).

6 At the command line enter **ATTDIA** <R> and:

prompt	New value for `ATTDIA<0>`
enter	**1** <R>.

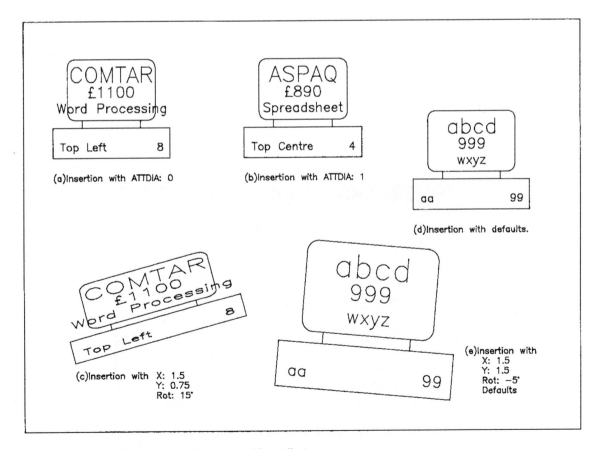

Figure 1.3 Investigating block insertion with attributes.

7 Select the Insert Block icon from the Draw toolbar and:

prompt	Insert dialogue box
with	COMPUTER as block name?
respond	pick OK
prompt	Insertion point and enter **150,180** <R>
prompt	X scale... and enter 1 <R>
prompt	Y scale... and enter 1 <R>
prompt	Rotation... and enter 0 <R>
prompt	Enter attributes dialogue box with prompts and defaults – Fig. 1.4
respond	alter the attribute values to:

    a)   What software?   Spreadsheet
    b)   Enter cost of computer   £890
    c)   Make of computer   ASPAQ
    d)   Position   Top Centre
    e)   Memory   4
    f)   pick OK.

8 The block is inserted as fig. (b).

9 Now decide on the method to add the attribute information to an inserted block:
    a) from keyboard – ATTDIA: 0
    b) from dialogue box – ATTDIA: 1.

Figure 1.4   Enter attributes dialogue box.

10 Insert the block COMPUTER with:
   a) `insertion point:` 35,45
   b) `X scale:` 1.5
   c) `Y scale:` 0.75
   d) `Rotation:` 15
   e) Attribute details as step 3.
   f) fig. (c).

11 Insert the block twice more with:

`insertion point`	265,145	170,30
`X scale`	1	1.5
`Y scale`	1	1.5
`rotation`	0	−5
attributes	defaults	defaults
	fig. (d)	fig. (e).

Displaying attributes

Attribute data which has been added to an inserted block can be 'turned off'. This is a useful option as the attribute information may not be for general viewing.

1 Select from the menu bar **Options**
                            Display
                            Attribute Display
                            Off

2 The five computer icons will be displayed with no attributes displayed.

3 At the command line enter **ATTDISP** <R> and:
   prompt   `Normal/ON/OFF<Off>`
   enter   **ON** <R>

4 The attribute data is re-displayed.

Exploding blocks with attributes

1 Select the EXPLODE icon from the Modify toolbar and pick the block at (a). The block will be exploded and it is the tags which will be displayed.

2 Repeat the explode command and select the other inserted blocks. All the blocks can be exploded.

3 *Note*. Previous AutoCAD releases have allowed uniform blocks ($X = Y$) to be exploded, but not non-uniform blocks. **Exploding non-uniform blocks is new to R13**.

4 Now erase all blocks, but do not exit the drawing.

Exercise

1 Refer to Fig. 1.5.

2 Create the window display for the six computer icons with all the attribute data from Fig. 1.1(a).

3 The block has to be inserted full size, i.e. $X = Y = 1$.

4 Select the attribute method of your choice, i.e. keyboard or dialogue box entry.

5 Add any other refinements to the window layout.

6 When the drawing is complete and all six blocks are inserted, save the layout as **C:\R13CUST\WINDOW** as it will be used in later chapters.

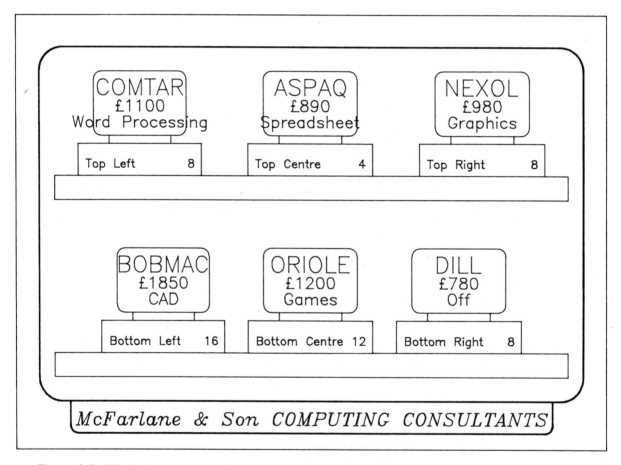

Figure 1.5 Window layout with attributes (save as R13CUST\WINDOW).

Summary

1 Attributes are text items attached to blocks and wblocks.

2 Blocks containing attributes are created and inserted in the usual manner.

3 Attributes are defined by a tag (label), a prompt and a default.

4 The ATTDIA variable allows attribute information to be entered:
  a) from the keyboard with ATTDIA 0
  b) from a dialogue box with ATTDIA 1.

5 Blocks with attributes can be inserted at varying *X* and *Y* scale factors and at varying rotation angles.

6 All blocks with attributes can be exploded.

7 Attributes attached to a block can be turned off with the ATTDISP command.

8 There are four attribute modes (constant; invisible; verify; preset) which have not been considered. Investigate these at your leisure.

Activity

Attribute examples usually involve quite a bit of keyboard entry, but there is no way to avoid this. I have included one attribute activity which has proved successful in my AutoCAD R12 and LT books. Lorries being loaded at a warehouse have a different load and destination and attributes have to be used to display all the information. The activity will be required for other chapters, so the complete drawing must be saved.

1 Use your STDA3 standard sheet.

2 Refer to Tutorial 1(a) and:
  a) draw a lorry icon using sizes in fig. (a)
  b) define the five attributes using the information in fig. (b)
  c) when the attributes are defined the lorry icon will be similar to fig. (c)
  d) make a block of the lorry and attributes. The block name should be LORRY, and I have given a suggested insertion point
  e) using the data given in fig. (d), insert the LORRY block and add all the attributes
  f) set the ATTDIA variable to suit.

3 When all the attributes have been added, the warehouse loading bay area should resemble Tutorial 1(b).

4 Save the completed drawing as:
  a) **C:\R13CUST\PARK** if you are using a named directory
  b) **A:PARK** if you use a floppy disk.

Editing attributes

Attributes which are attached to blocks can be edited to correct errors or alter existing values. To demonstrate the editing of attributes, we will continue with our computer shop window layout.

The owner of the computer shop is concerned about his poor recent sales figures ever since a new superstore opened in a nearby business park. He has thus decided to reduce the price of some of the computers in the window by having a sale. The sale prices are:

COMTAR	£654
ASPAQ	£456
NEXOL	£650
DILL	£357 and displaying an Accounts package.

Editing single attribute blocks

1 Open your C:\R13CUST\WINDOW drawing created in the previous chapter.

2 Display the Attribute toolbar.

3 Select the Edit Attribute icon from the Attribute and:
   prompt   Select block
   respond   pick the top left block then right-click
   prompt   Edit Attributes dialogue box – looks familiar?
   respond   *a*) alter **£1100** to **!! £654 !!**
         b) pick OK.

4 Using the Edit Attribute icon, select the appropriate block and alter the cost values of the following attributes:
   ASPAQ   to !! £456 !!
   NEXOL   to !! £650 !!
   DILL   to !! £357 !! with Accounts Package.

5 When the attributes have all been edited, the window layout resembles Fig. 2.1.

6 Save this layout if required but **NOT AS WINDOW**.

7 Do not exit the drawing.

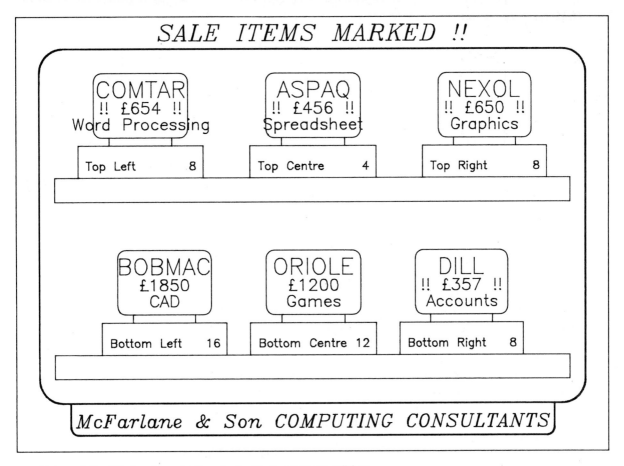

Figure 2.1 Window layout after single block attribute editing.

Global attribute editing

Single attribute editing is very useful but the process can be very tedious if the drawing contains several attributes which require editing. It is possible to edit attributes globally by specifying:

a) the attribute block name
b) the tag
c) the value of the attribute.

Editing by tag

The shop owner wants to change the text style of the computer name as well as the height of the RAM memory displayed on the icons. The text style he has selected is one of the sanserrif types, and the RAM memory height is to be increased to 10.

1 Continue with the window layout.

2 Create a new text style called **ATT** from the **sasb_pfb** font and accept all the defaults including the 0 height.

3 Select the Edit Attributes Globally icon from the Attribute toolbar and:

prompt	`Edit attributes one at a time?<Y>`
enter	**Y** <R>
prompt	`Block name specification<*>`
respond	right-click
prompt	`Attribute tag specification<*>`
enter	**MAKE** <R>
prompt	`Attribute value specification<*>`
respond	right-click
prompt	`Select Attributes`
respond	window the complete layout then right-click
prompt	`6 attributes selected` - true?
then	`Value/Position/Height...`
	and an **X** appears at one of the make values (my layout had the X at DILL)
enter	**S** <R> – the style option
prompt	`Text style: STDA3`
then	New style or RETURN for no change
enter	**ATT** <R>
prompt	`Value/Position/Height...` and DILL text style altered
enter	**N** <R> – the next option and the X moves to another MAKE value
prompt	`Value/Position/Height...`
enter	**S** <R>
prompt	`New style...`
enter	**ATT** <R> then `Value/Position/Height...`
respond	*a*) continue with the N option
	b) enter **S** for style change
	c) enter **ATT** as the new style.
	d) repeat **N** and **S** until all the MAKE text styles have been altered.

4 *Exercise*
a) Use the ATTEDIT command and specify the tag specification RAM.
b) Alter all memory heights to 10.

Editing by value

A specific attribute value can be altered with the ATTEDIT command and we will demonstrate this by altering two of the window layout values:

a) Word Processing has been replaced with a Database package.

b) The 8 RAM machines have all been upgraded to 10 RAM.

1 Altered window layout still on screen?

2 At the command line enter **ATTEDIT** <R> and:

prompt	`Edit attributes one at a time` and right-click
prompt	`Block name specification` and right-click
prompt	`Attribute tag specification` and right-click
prompt	`Attribute value specification<*>`
enter	**Word Processing** <R>
prompt	`Select Attributes`
respond	window the display then right-click
prompt	`1 attribute selected` and X at Word Processing
prompt	`Value/Position/Height...`
enter	**V** <R> – the value option
prompt	`Change or Replace`
enter	**R** <R> – the replace option
prompt	`New attribute value`
enter	**Database** <R>
prompt	`Value/Position...`
respond	right-click.

3 Using the ATTEDIT command:

a) enter an attribute value specification of **8**

b) window the layout

c) use the (V)alue, (R)eplace options and enter 10 at the highlighted (X) attributes.

Partial attribute editing

This option is obtained by responding **N** to the first prompt of the ATTEDIT command, and allows parts of the attribute value to be altered.

1 Activate the Edit Attributes Globally command and:

prompt	`Edit attributes one at a time`
enter	**N** `<R>`
prompt	`Global edit if attribute values` then `Edit only attributes visible on screen<Y>`
enter	**Y** `<R>`
prompt	Block name spec and right-click
prompt	Attribute tag spec and right-click
prompt	Attribute value spec and right-click
prompt	`Select Attributes`
respond	window the display then right-click
prompt	`30 attributes selected`
then	`String to change`
enter	**Top** `<R>`
prompt	`New string`
enter	**T** `<R>`

2 All blocks on the top shelf will be displayed with the attribute position value as T Left, etc.

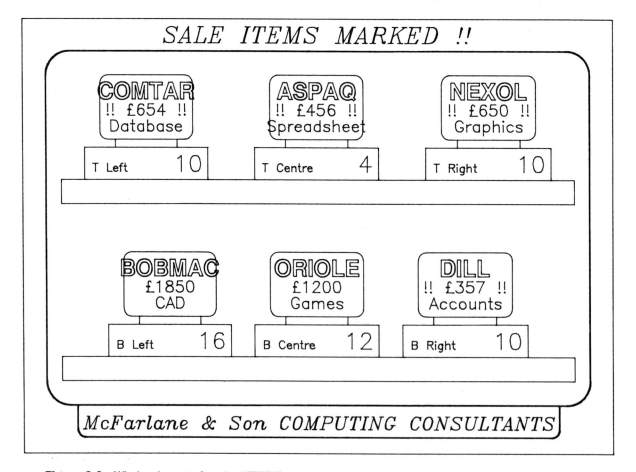

Figure 2.2   Window layout after the ATTEDIT command.

3 Use the ATTEDIT command again (entering **N** at the first prompt) and alter the string Bottom to B.

4 At this stage your drawing of the window display should resemble Fig. 2.2 and can be saved as the edit attributes exercise is now complete. ***Do not save as WINDOW***.

5 Do not quit the drawing.

DDEDIT

Most AutoCAD users will have used the dynamic edit command (DDEDIT) to alter existing text on the screen. The command also allows attribute tags to be altered.

1 From the menu bar select **Modify**
　　　　　　　　Edit Text...
prompt　　`<Select an annotation object>...`
respond　pick any attribute text item and nothing happens
respond　right-click.

2 Explode any block to display the attribute tags.

3 Repeat the Modify-Edit Text sequence and pick the MAKE text item from the exploded block and:
prompt　　`Edit Attribute Definition` dialogue box – Fig. 2.3.

4 This dialogue box allows the tag, prompt and defaults entries to be edited for the selected tag.

5 Cancel the dialogue box then right-click.

6 You can now exit AutoCAD.

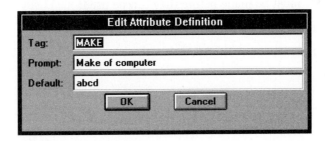

Figure 2.3 Edit attribute definition dialogue box.

Summary

1 Single blocks with attributes attached can be edited with the Edit Attribute icon.
2 The ATTEDIT command and the Edit Attributes Globally icon allow editing:
　　a) by block name
　　b) by tag
　　c) by value.
3 Global editing has several options and allows the value; position; height; angle; style; layer and colour of an attribute value to be altered.
4 Global editing also allows individual 'strings' of an attribute to be altered.

Activity

The activity for this chapter involves the warehouse loading bay with the lorries from Chapter 1.

Tutorial 2

The shipping clerk has made several mistakes with the loading and these have to be corrected with attribute editing. This will involve both individual and global editing.

1 Open the PARK drawing from Chapter 1.

2 The editing is as follows:

  a) lorry A123 ROW has been rerouted to NEWCASTLE with COAL

  b) driver B.SLOW was held up in traffic and has been replaced with driver G.O.FAST.

  c) no BOWLER HATS were available for the lorry to LONDON, and it was loaded with CONFECTIONERY

  d) the lorries in bays 6 and 7 had their loads mixed up.

3 Other alterations were:

  a) all destinations should be in ITALIC TRIPLEX text style with a height of 5

  b) all loads should be in the SASBO_PFB text style, height 6

  c) all drivers names should be in red

  d) all registration numbers should be in green.

  e) all 2's should be TWO's.

  Note: the two text styles must be made before they can be used!

4 When all editing is complete, the loading bay should resemble Tutorial 2.

5 Save the completed edited layout as **PARK-A**.

Chapter 3

Extracting attribute data from a drawing

Attributes which are attached to blocks in a drawing usually contain information which could be used in other software packages, e.g. databases and spreadsheets. AutoCAD R13 allows attribute information to be extracted from a drawing in three formats, these being:

1 Comma Delimited File (CDF): the extracted attribute data is separated with commas. Quotation marks " " are placed around alphanumeric data, but not around numeric data.

2 Space Delimited File (SDF): this extract file format has the data spaced out into field widths.

3 Drawing Interchange File (DXF): is the format most easily read by other CAD systems as well as CNC systems. It can be difficult to read by the user.

Note

1 The file format to be extracted will depend on what software package the attribute data is to be used with. Some packages prefer the CDF type format, while others require the data to be in fields – hence the SDF format.

2 The DXF format is a 'universal standard' and is generally used with other CAD systems as well as CNC and CAM.

Template file

Attribute data which is to be extracted from a drawing in CDF or SDF format requires a set of instructions on how and what information is to be extracted. These instructions are obtained by the user writing a **template file** – an AutoCAD phrase. The attribute data which is being extracted requires to be 'stored' in an extract file. When extracting attribute data, the user is therefore working with three different files:

1 the drawing file containing the attribute information

2 the template file to extract the attribute data

3 the extract file to 'store' the extracted data.

Note

1 The template file is a text file with the extension **.txt** and is written by the user.

2 The extract file is also a text file with the extension **.txt**. It is automatically created by AutoCAD, but the user assigns a name to the file.

3 The general interaction between the drawing/template/extract files is displayed in Fig. 3.1(a).

4 Template files can be written using any text editor. We will use the MS DOS text editor from within AutoCAD. This will enable us to use AutoCAD's external commands.

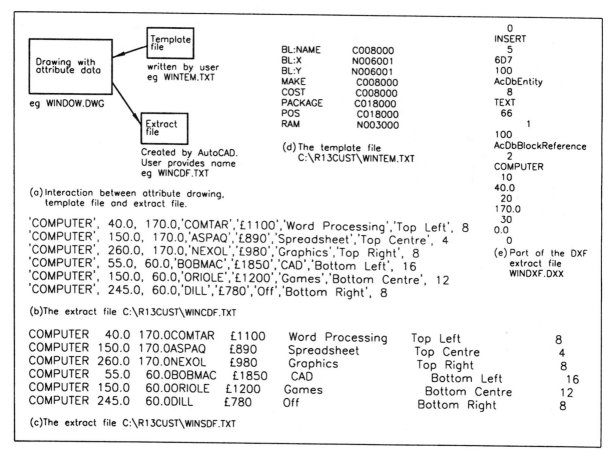

Figure 3.1 Template and extract files.

Creating a template file

For our attribute extract exercise, we will return to the computer shop window layout. The shop owner wants a detailed list of the items in the window, and we will supply this as attribute data extract files. The template file has to be written so:

1 Open the window layout drawing **c:\R13CUST\WINDOW** created in Chapter 1. This layout should display six computer icons with the original attribute data.

2 At the command line enter **SHELL** <R> and:

prompt   OS Command
enter   **EDIT C:\R13CUST\WINTEM.TXT** <R> – note full file name
prompt   MS DOS text editor screen with WINTEM.TXT name
respond   enter the following lines but:
Note: *a)* ensure the C and N entries **START AT COLUMN 13**
      b) DO NOT RETURN AT THE LAST LINE.

The lines to enter are:

BL:NAME   **C008000**<R>
BL:X   **N006001**<R>
BL:Y   **N006001**<R>
MAKE   **C008000**<R>
COST   **C008000**<R>
PACKAGE   **C018000**<R>
POS   **C018000**<R>
RAM   **N003000** – NO RETURN

3 From the menu bar select **File–Save As...** and:
prompt   Save As dialogue box
respond   *a)* check directory is C:\R13CUST
      b) check file name is WINTEM.TXT
      c) pick OK.

4 From the menu bar select **File-Exit** to return to the AutoCAD screen with the window layout drawing.

Explanation of template file

Before proceeding with the attribute extract exercise, it is worthwhile explaining the layout of the template file, as it will probably be new to most users.

1 The template file name is C:\R13CUST\WINTEM.TXT.
  a) the C:\ is for the hard drive
  b) R13CUST is our directory name on the hard drive
  c) WINTEM.TXT is **MY** template file name from:
    WIN – reference to the window layout drawing
    TEM – used to indicate a template file
    .TXT – is the file extension and **IS ESSENTIAL**.

2 The first three lines of the file begin with **BL:**. This allows information about blocks to be extracted and:
  a) BL:NAME – is for the block name
  b) BL:X – is for the X co-ordinate of the insertion point
  c) BL:Y – is for the Y co-ordinate of the insertion point.
  Other block information can be extracted, e.g. scale factors, rotation angle, but the three listed are the most common.

3 The C008000, N006001, etc. refer to the **type** of attribute data being extracted and each is divided into three sections:

  C|008|000 and N|006|001

  a) C: is for alpha-numeric extract data, e.g. COMTAR, £1100, etc.
  b) 008: is the 'length' of the data being extracted
  c) 000: all alpha-numerics have 000 as the last three digits
  d) N: refers to numeric data only, e.g. 16, 165.0, etc.
  e) 006: is the numeric data 'length' and includes the decimal point
  f) 001: the numeric data will have one decimal place
  g) thus:

    C018000 is a character field of length 18
    N003000 is a numeric field of length 3 with no decimal places, i.e. whole numbers.

4 To determine the length of the field, count the number of digits and/or letters of the largest **value** to be used with the particular tag. You can also add one or two extra digits.

5 The lines MAKE, COST, PACKAGE, etc. are the attribute tag names which have to be extracted and **must be identical to the tags in the block definition**.

6 I recommend that the template file be stored in the same directory as the drawing from which attributes are to be extracted.

7 Never use the tab key when writing the template file. Add spaces with the space bar.

8 End each line of the template file with <RETURN> with the exception of the last line. After the last line has been written **DO NOT PRESS THE RETURN KEY**.

9 The C and N entries **must begin at column 13**.

Extracting the attribute information

Once the template file has been written and saved, it can be used to extract the attribute information added to the blocks.

1 Window layout still on screen?

2 At the command line enter **ATTEXT** <R> and:
   prompt   CDF, SDF or DXF Attribute extraction<C>
   enter   **C** <R> – for CDF format
   prompt   Select Template File dialogue box
   respond   *a*) check directory is c:\r13cust
          b) pick **wintem.txt**
          c) pick OK
   prompt   Create Extract File dialogue box
   respond   *a*) check directory is c:\r13cust
          b) enter file name as **wincdf.txt**
          c) pick OK.

3 If the template file has been written correctly, and if there are no errors in the attribute blocks, then:

   prompt   6 records in extract file.

4 This means that the extraction process has been successful, but nothing appears to have happened.

5 The SDF format can be extracted in a similar manner, but we will use the attribute extraction dialogue box, so at the command line enter **DDATTEXT** <R> and:
   prompt   Attribute Extraction dialogue box
   respond   *a*) pick SDF format
          b) pick Template File...
          c) pick **wintem.txt** then OK
          d) pick Output File...
          e) enter file name as **winsdf.txt** then OK
          f) pick Select Objects <
   prompt   Select objects
   respond   window the layout then right-click
   prompt   Attribute Extraction dialogue box as Fig. 3.2
   respond   pick OK.

6 All being well – six records in extract file, but still nothing appears to have happened.

7 The DXF format is extracted in a slightly different way from the CDF and SDF formats – a template file is not required. At the command line enter **ATTEXT** <R> and:
   prompt   CDF, SDF or DXF.....
   enter   **D** <R>
   prompt   Create extract file dialogue box
   respond   enter file name as **windxf** then pick OK
   prompt   42(?) objects in extract file and drawing screen returned.

8 A DXF attribute extract file is not a **.txt** file. It is given the extension **.dxx** which is a 'compiled' file.

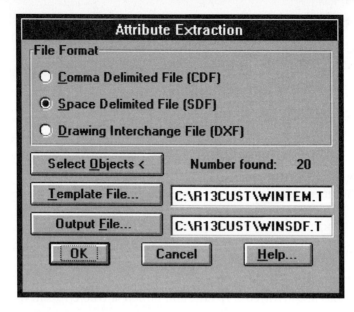

Figure 3.2 Attribute extraction dialogue box.

Attribute extraction errors

While extracting attributes appears to be relatively simple, errors usually happen the first time that the ATTEXT command is used. The most common error is 'invalid field specification'. The errors are generally in the template file, and the most common are:
a) using the letter O instead of the number 0
b) using N instead of C for an alpha-numeric field
c) entering a <RETURN> at the last line
d) not starting the C and N entries at column 13.

Viewing the extract files

Attribute extract files can be viewed:
a) from the MS DOS text editor
b) by importing the files into AutoCAD.

1 Still in AutoCAD?

2 At the command line enter **SHELL** <R> and:
   prompt   OS Command
   enter   **EDIT C:\R13CUST\WINSDF.TXT** <R>
   prompt   DOS editor with SDF attribute extract file displayed. Is the displayed data correct?

3 Now select File–Exit from the menu bar. Using the SHELL–EDIT entry method as above allows any extract file to be viewed.

4 Open your STDA3 standard sheet.

5 Select the **Text** icon from the Draw toolbar and:
   prompt   Attach/.....<Insert point>
   enter   **10,260** <R>
   prompt   Attach/.....<Other corner>
   enter   **330,180** <R>
   prompt   Edit MText dialogue box

respond	pick **Import...**
prompt	Import Text File dialogue box
respond	a) double left-click on **r13cust** directory
	b) alter file name to ***.txt** then \<R>
	c) pick **wincdf.txt** file name
	d) pick OK
prompt	Edit MText dialogue box with wincdf.txt file displayed
respond	pick OK.

6 The wincdf.txt attribute extract text file will be positioned as required on the drawing – Fig. 3.1(b).

Note: the first time I used the MText command I had to pick a font file name to allow the import.

7 Repeat the Text icon selection and:
a) enter 10,190 as the insert point
b) enter 370,120 as the other corner point
c) import the winsdf.txt file then OK
d) pick OK from the Edit MText dialogue box
e) file is imported – Fig. 3.1(c).

8 *Task:* Can you import the wintem.txt template file – Fig. 3.1(d).

9 To view the DXF format extract file enter **SHELL** \<R> and:

prompt	OS Command
enter	**EDIT C:\R13CUST\WINDXF.DXX** \<R>
prompt	text editor displays the extract file. This file will display numbers and words which may be familiar to the user but will probably not mean anything. You may recognize some of the numbers
respond	a) examine the file
	b) pick File–Exit from the command line.

10 I have included part of the windxf.dxx extract file in Fig. 3.1(e).

Summary

1 Attribute data can be extracted from a drawing in three formats:
a) Comma Delimited File (CDF)
b) Space Delimited File (SDF)
c) Drawing Interchange File (DXF).

2 The CDF and SDF formats are suitable for importing into packages such as databases and spreadsheets. The DXF format is used with other CAD systems and CNC/CAM systems.

3 Both the CDF and SDF extract formats require a template file to be used. This template file must be written by the user. It is a text file with the extension .txt.

4 Template files are written using any text editor.

5 The CDF and SDF extract files are .txt files. The user names these extract files.

6 Extracting CDF and SDF attribute data involves three files:
a) the drawing file (.DWG) containing the attributes
b) the template file (.TXT)
c) the extract file (.TXT).

7 The DXF extract file has the extension .DXX. This is a compiled file and can prove to be difficult to 'read'.

8 All text files can be imported into AutoCAD with the MTEXT command or by selecting the TEXT icon.

Activity

The attribute extraction activity will involve the original lorry loading bay activity from Chapter 1 – saved as PARK?

Tutorial 3

The attribute entered on the lorries has to be extracted in both CDF and SDF format, and will necessitate a template file. As attribute extraction is a new concept, I have included the extract file, which should be written from within AutoCAD with:

a) SHELL

    EDIT ....

The file is:	BL:NAME	C008000 <R>
	BL:X	N006001 <R>
	BL:Y	N006001 <R>
	REG	C010000 <R>
	DEST	C012000 <R>
	DRIV	C008000 <R>
	LOAD	C012000 <R>
	BAY	N002000 NO RETURN

b) My suggestions for the file names are:

template: C:\R13CUST\PARKTEM.TXT
CDF format: PARKCDF.TXT
SDF format: PARKSDF.TXT.

c) As an exercise. I imported both extract files into the PARK drawing as shown in Tutorial 3. The original layout was scaled by a factor of 0.5.

Chapter 4

External references

Blocks contain information about entities, colour, layers, linetypes, etc., and all this information is inserted into the drawing with the block. This uses memory. Drawings which contain several blocks are not automatically updated if one of the original block drawings is modified. External references (or **Xrefs**) are similar to blocks in that they can be inserted into a drawing, but they have one major advantage. Drawings which contain external references are automatically updated if the external reference 'block' is modified.

External references will be demonstrated by worked examples. The procedure will appear to be rather involved as it requires the user to open and save several times, but the final result is well worth the time and effort spend, so persevere with the exercise. For the demonstration we will:
a) create two external references
b) use these Xrefs in two drawings
c) modify the external references
d) view the original drawings
e) investigate the external references.

Creating the Xrefs

1 Start AutoCAD Release 13.

2 From the menu bar select **File–New** and:
a) leave the Prototype drawing name
b) enter **C:\R13CUST\XX1** as the new drawing name
c) pick OK.

3 Make a new layer XREF1, colour blue and current.

4 Refer to Fig. 4.1 and draw a 20 unit square with both diagonals.

5 At the command line enter **BASE** <R> and:
prompt   Base point<0,0,0>
respond   INTersection and pick the diagonal intersection

6 From the menu bar select **File-Save** to automatically save the blue square as C:\R13CUST\XX1.

7 From the menu bar select File–New and:
a) leave the Prototype name
b) enter new drawing name as **C:\R13CUST\XX2**
c) pick OK.

8 Make a new layer XREF2, colour green and current.

9 With the snap on, draw a polygon:
a) with six sides
b) centre at a snap point
c) inscribed in a 25 radius circle.

10 At the command line:
   a) enter **BASE** <R>
   b) pick the polygon 'snap centre'.

11 From the menu bar select **File-Save** to automatically save the green hexagonal as
C:\R13CUST\XX2.

12 *Note*. We have: *a*) created two drawings XX1 and XX2
   b) set a base point relative to the square and hexagon to assist with
   the Xref insertion.

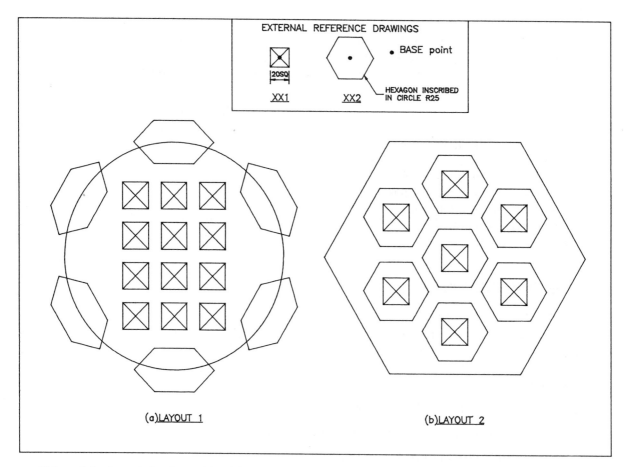

Figure 4.1 Layout drawings with original XREFS attached.

Drawing 1

1 Begin a **New** drawing with:
   a) prototype name: C:\R13CUST\STDA3
   b) new drawing name: C:\R13CUST\LAYOUT1.

2 Display the Draw, Modify, Object Snap and External Reference toolbars.

3 With layer OUT (red) current, draw a circle of radius 85 with its centre at 190,135.

4 Select the Attach icon from the external Reference toolbar and:

   prompt   Select file to attach dialogue box
   respond *a*) double left-click on r13cust directory
            b) pick xx1.dwg drawing file
            c) pick OK.
   prompt   Attach Xref XX1: XX1.DWG
            XX1 loaded
            Insertion point
   enter   **160,180** <R>
   prompt   X scale... and enter **1** <R>
   prompt   Y scale... and enter **1** <R>
   prompt   Rotation... and enter **0** <R>

5 The blue XX1 square is displayed.

6 Rectangular array the blue square:
   a) for four rows and three columns
   b) row distance: −30
   c) column distance: 30

7 At the command line enter **XREF** <R> and:
   prompt   ?/Bind/...../<Attach>
   enter   **A** <R> – the attach option
   prompt   Select file to attach dialogue box
   respond *a*) double left-click on r13cust directory
            b) pick xx2.dwg drawing file
            c) pick OK.
   prompt   Attach Xref XX2: XX2.DWG
            XX2 loaded
            Insertion point
   respond **QUAdrant and pick top of red circle**
   prompt   X scale... and enter **1.25** <R>
   prompt   Y scale... and enter **0.75** <R>
   prompt   Rotation... and enter **0** <R>.

8 The green XX2 hexagon is displayed.

9 Polar array the green hexagon:
   a) about the red circle centre
   b) for six items, full circle with rotation.

10 Layout resembles Fig. 4.1(a).

11 Select from the menu bar **File–Save** to automatically save the drawing as C:\R13CUST\LAYOUT1.

Investigating the Xrefs

1 At the command line enter **BLOCK** <R> and:

prompt	Block name (or ?)
enter	**?** <R>
prompt	Block(s) to list<*>
respond	right-click
prompt	Text screen with:

Defined blocks
XX1   Xref: resolved
XX2   Xref: resolved

User	External	Dependent	Unnamed
Blocks	References	Blocks	Blocks
0	2	0	0

2 Flip back to the drawing screen with F2.

3 Select the List icon from the External Reference toolbar and:

prompt	?/Bind/..... then Xref(s) to list<*>
respond	right-click
prompt	Text screen with:

Xref name	Path	Xref type
XX1	XX1.DWG	Attach
XX2	XX2.DWG	Attach
Total Xref(s): 2		

4 F2 to return to the drawing screen.

5 Activate the layer control dialogue box and note the two new layers:
XX1|XREF1   blue
XX2|XREF2   green

Note:	*a)* XREF1 and XREF2 are the two new layers
	b)	is a pipe symbol and indicates that XX1 has been created on layer XREF1.
	Pipe symbols (|) are used to indicate non-graphical information.

6 Cancel the dialogue box.

7 Select the Path icon from the External Reference toolbar and:

prompt	?/Bind/.....
then	Edit path for which xref(s)
enter	**XX1** <R>
prompt	Scanning...
	Xref name: XX1
	Old path: XX1.DWG
	New path:
respond	**ESCAPE** to exit command.
prompt	Path unchanged.

8 Proceed to the next section – have you saved the layout?

Drawing 2

1 Begin a new drawing with:
a) prototype name: C:\R13CUST\STDA3
b) new drawing name: C:\R13CUST\LAYOUT2.

2 With layer OUT (red) current, draw a polygon:
a) with six sides
b) centred on 190,135
c) inscribed in a circle of radius 20.

3 Attach external reference XX1 full size with zero rotation at the following points:

a) 145,165   b) 190,190   c) 235,165   d) 145,110   e) 190,135   f) 235,110
g) 190,80.

4 Attach external reference XX2 at the same seven points as step 3, full size with zero rotation.

5 The result will be Fig. 4.1(b).

6 Select File–Save to automatically update C:\R13CUST\LAYOUT2.

Modifying the Xrefs

1 Open drawing XX1 and erase the blue object.

2 Draw two concentric circles of radii 10 and 20 with layer XREF1 current. Change the colour of the two circles to green.

3 Set BASE to the circle centres.

4 Select File–Save to update XX1.

5 Open drawing XX2 and erase the green polygon.

6 Create the following text style:

Name: XREF
Font: sasbo_.pfb
Ht: 15 and accept the other defaults.

7 Draw the text phrase CAD, centred on any suitable point and change its colour to blue.

8 Set the BASE to the text phrase centre point.

9 Select File–Save to update XX2.

Viewing the drawing layouts

1 Open drawing LAYOUT1 and note that the Preview displays the original blue square and green hexagon, then:

prompt   `Resolve Xref  XX1: XX1.DWG`
       `XX1 loaded`
       `Resolve Xref  XX2: XX2.DWG`
       `XX2 loaded`

2 The layout 1 drawing will be displayed with the modified external references, i.e. the green circles and blue text items – Fig. 4.2(a).

3 Check the layer control dialogue box. XX1|XREF1 and XX2|XREF2?

4 Select File–Save to update drawing XX1.

5 Open drawing LAYOUT2 which will be displayed as Fig. 4.2(b), i.e. with the modified external references.

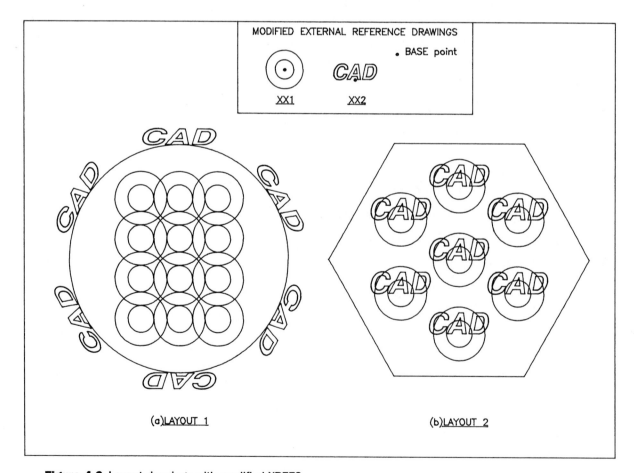

Figure 4.2 Layout drawings with modified XREFS.

6 Select the Overlay icon from the External Reference toolbar and:

prompt   `Select file to overlay` dialogue box

respond   *a*) double left-click on r13cust directory

            b) pick layout1.dwg file

            c) pick OK

prompt   `Overlay Xref LAYOUT1: LAYOUT1.DWG`

            `Block XX1 previously resolved. Definition ignored`

            `Block XX2 previously resolved. Definition ignored.`

            `LAYOUT1 loaded`

            `then   Insertion point`

prompt   `200,100 <R>`

prompt   `X scale...` and enter **1** `<R>`

prompt   `Y scale...` and enter **1** `<R>`

prompt   `Rotation...` and enter **0** `<R>`.

7 Zoom-all to display both layout drawings with the modified external references.

8 Activate the layer control dialogue box and note several new pipe LAYOUT1 layers.

9 Select the List icon from the External Reference toolbar and:

prompt   `Xref(s) to list` and right-click

prompt   Text screen with:

Xref name	Path	Xref type
LAYOUT1	LAYOUT1.DWG	Overlay
XX1	XX1.DWG	Attach
XX2	XX2.DWG	Attach

10 Flip back to the drawing screen then proceed to the next section.

Binding Xrefs

1 Re-open drawing LAYOUT2, pick **No** to the save drawing changes.

2 At the command line enter **XREF** `<R>` and:

prompt   `?/Bind/Detach/.....`

enter   **B** `<R>` – the bind option

prompt   `Xref(s) to bind`

enter   **XX1,XX2** `<R>`

prompt   `Scanning...`

3 Activate the layer control dialogue box and note layers:

XX1$0$XREF1   blue

XX2$0$XREF2   green

Note: The pipe symbol (|) has been replaced by **0** indicating that the layer contains a bound xref and is no longer attached.

4 Select File–Save to update LAYOUT2.

Modifying the Xrefs (again)

1 Open drawing XX1 and draw a blue donut, centred at 300,100 with ID 15 and OD 20.

2 Erase the green circles.

3 Set the BASE at the donut centre then File-Save to update XX1.

4 Open drawing XX2 and draw a green rectangle with length 60 and breadth 20. Use the snap on.

5 Erase the blue text item and set the BASE at the rectangle 'centre' point.

6 Select File–Save to update XX2.

7 Open drawing LAYOUT1 to display the layout with the donuts and rectangles.

8 Open drawing LAYOUT2 to display the green circles and blue text items, i.e. the modified Xrefs have not been updated due to the bind effect.

9 This completes the external reference exercise.

Summary

1 External references (Xrefs) are similar in usage to blocks.
2 Xrefs can be attached to drawings.
3 If an Xref is modified, all drawings which has the Xref attached is automatically updated to include the modification.
4 Xrefs can be 'bound' to a drawing. When bound they cease to be external references and will not be updated.
5 This has been a brief introduction to external referencing to demonstrate the 'power' of the concept.

Chapter 5

Customizing linetypes

AutoCAD Release 13 has several pre-defined linetypes which should have been loaded into your STDA3 standard sheet. Most users should know how linetypes are generally used with layers and how their appearance is controlled by the LTSCALE command, which was set to 12 in our STDA3 standard sheet. While the AutoCAD linetypes are usually more than sufficient for normal draughting requirements, there may be the odd occasion when it is necessary to create new linetypes.

AutoCAD R13 allows three types of line to be created:

a) simple: consisting of dashes, dots and spaces,
   e.g. ___...___...___...___...
b) complex: with text items added,
   e.g. ___ME___ME___ME
c) complex: with shape items added,
   e.g. ___>< ___>< ___><

In this chapter we will investigate how to create linetypes *a*) and *b*) and leave the complex *c*) type until we have investigated shapes.

What are linetypes?

A linetype consists of a series of dashes, spaces and dots, spaced out according to a predefined pattern. AutoCAD linetypes are contained in the **ACAD.LIN** file which is a text file within the SUPPORT sub-directory. To view the existing linetype file:

1 Start AutoCAD and open your STDA3 standard sheet.

2 At the command line enter **SHELL** <R> and:
   prompt   OS Command
   enter   **EDIT C:\R13\COM\SUPPORT\ACAD.LIN** <R>
             (*Note*: R13 is MY directory for Release 13)
   prompt   MS text editor displaying the ACAD.LIN file.

3 Scroll down the file and note the various linetype definitions, two of which are:
   a) *BORDER,__ __ . __ __ . __ __ .
      A,.5,−.25,.5,−.25,0,−.25
   b) *CENTER,_____ _ _____ _ _____ _
      A,1.25,−.25,.25,−.25

4 Exit the ACAD.LIN file with **File–Exit** from the menu bar to return to the drawing screen.

Linetype descriptors

Every linetype in a .LIN file has a two line **DESCRIPTOR** consisting of three distinct parts:

1 The name of the linetype preceded by an asterisk (*), e.g. *CENTER. The name should be in CAPITALS.

2 A graphical description of the linetype which *is not to scale*. This is made of dashes (_), dots (.) and spaces entered from the keyboard. It follows on from the linetype name, and is *separated from the name by a comma (,)*.

3 The actual linetype pattern line which is a coded definition of the linetype in a form which can be interpreted by a plotter, e.g. pen down and pen up movements. The actual values are *drawing units*. The coded definition for the CENTER linetype is A,1.25,−.25,.25, −.25 which can be interpreted as:
   a) the **A,** is an 'alignment field' and is **ESSENTIAL**, i.e. every second line must begin with A,
   b) 1.25 means a pen down movement of 1.25 drawing units
   c) −.25 means a pen up movement of .25 drawing units
   d) .25 is a pen down movement of .25 drawing units
   e) −.25 is a pen up movement of .25 drawing units.

Notes

1 A positive pattern line number signifies pen down, i.e. a line.

2 A negative pattern number means pen up, i.e. no line (a space).

3 A zero pattern line number gives a dot.

4 A drawing unit is 1 mm.

5 The linetype 'appearance' is controlled by the LTSCALE variable.

6 The linetype descriptor has a very strict format and the syntax is important. The format *cannot be altered* and is:

*NAME, dashes-dots-spaces
A, pen down and pen up movements

7 The actual number of pen movements in the second line need only be specified until the **REPEAT PATTERN** is completely defined, i.e. 1.25,−.25,.25,−.25 is the complete repeat pattern for the CENTER linetype.

8 The dash-dot-space description can be replaced with a written text item, e.g. use for centre lines. The text should *not exceed 47 characters*. The comma is still essential between the linetype name and the written description.

9 The pen down and pen up movements *cannot exceed 12 in total*.

10 Figure 5.1(A) details the two linetypes (BORDER and CENTER) from the ACAD.LIN file and displays:
   a) the linetype repeat pattern with sizes as drawing units
   b) the two complete linetype descriptors
   c) the linetype appearance at different LTSCALE values.

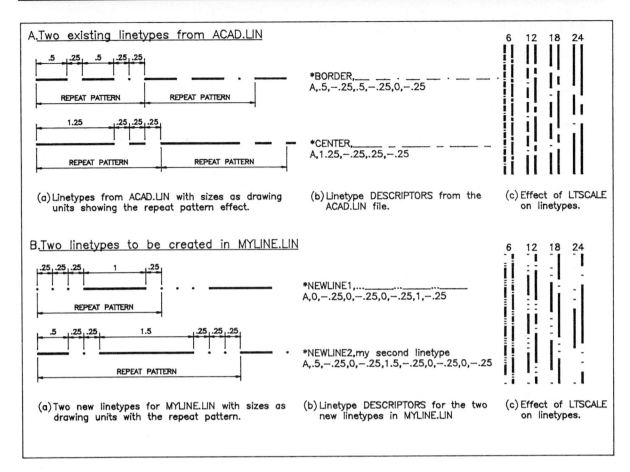

Figure 5.1 Linetype definitions, descriptors and appearance.

Customizing two new simple linetypes

Linetypes are stored in text files which have the extension **.LIN** and AutoCAD allows new linetypes to be created:

1 within the existing ACAD.LIN file
2 in user defined .LIN files.

In our investigation, we will create linetypes in a new file which we will call MYLINE. This will ensure that the original ACAD.LIN file remains untouched – a wise precaution?

There are two methods for customizing linetypes:
a) from within AutoCAD using the LINETYPE command
b) by using a text editor either externally or from AutoCAD itself.

We will create a linetype by each method. Fig. 5.1(B) displays these linetypes, detailing:
a) the linetype repeat pattern with drawing unit sizes
b) the complete linetype descriptors
c) the linetype appearance at different LTSCALE values.

a) Using the LINETYPE command

1 Clear your drawing screen of any entities.

2 At the command line enter **LINETYPE** <R> and:

prompt	?/Create/Load/Set
enter	**C** <R> – the create option
prompt	Name of linetype to create
enter	**NEWLINE1** <R>
prompt	Create or Append Linetype File
with	acad as the file name
respond	*a*) pick the r13cust directory
	b) enter file name as **MYLINE**
	c) pick OK
prompt	Creating new file
then	Descriptive text
enter	...____...____...____ <R>
prompt	A,
enter	**0,–.25,0,–.25,0,–.25,1,–.25** <R>
prompt	New definition written to file
then	?/Create/Load/Set
respond	right-click to cancel command.

b) Using a text editor

1 Still in AutoCAD with your STDA3 standard sheet – blank?

2 At the command line enter **SHELL** <R> and:

prompt	OS Command
enter	**EDIT C:\R13CUST\MYLINE.LIN** <R>
prompt	MS DOS Editor
with	*NEWLINE1 definition

(Note: you may have a 'title page' line as well as the two line definition – this is OK).

respond	*a*) move cursor below last line of text
	b) enter the following lines:

       *NEWLINE2,my second linetype <R>
       A,.5,–.25,0,–.25,1.5,–.25,0,–.25,0,–.25 <R>.

3 From the menu bar select **File–Save As** and:
a) check directory C:\R13CUST
b) check file name MYLINE.LIN
c) pick OK.

4 From the menu bar select **File–Exit** to leave the text editor and return to the AutoCAD drawing screen.

Loading the new linetypes

The two new created linetypes have to be loaded before they can be used, so:

1 At the command line enter **LINETYPE** <R> and:

prompt	`?/Create.....`
enter	**L** <R> – the load option
prompt	`Linetype(s) to load`
enter	***** <R> – wildcard for all
prompt	`Select Linetype File` dialogue box
respond	*a*) double left-click on the r13cust directory
	b) pick myline.lin file
	c) pick OK
prompt	`Linetype NEWLINE1 loaded`
	`Linetype NEWLINE2 loaded`
then	`?/Create.....`
enter	**?** <R>
prompt	`Select Linetype File` dialogue box
with	`myline as file name?`
respond	pick **OK**
prompt	Text screen with:

```
Linetypes defined in file C:\R13CUST\MYLINE.lin
Name       Description
NEWLINE1   ..._____..._____..._____
NEWLINE2   my second linetype
```

respond	F2 to toggle back to the drawing screen.
prompt	`?/Create...`
respond	right-click to end the command.

2 *Note.* If there are any errors in your created linetypes a message will be displayed. The message 'Bad definition ...' is the most common and is usually a result of (*a*) commas being omitted, (*b*) full-stops being used instead of commas, (*c*) no positive/negative sequence.

To correct the errors, enter the text editor (SHELL–EDIT, etc.) and view the written linetype file. Correct any apparent errors.

Using the new linetypes

We left the computer shop owner with a sale. This sale resulted in all the stock being sold, and the shop owner moved his premises to a new shopping complex in a re-developed area. It is this shopping area which will be drawn using our new linetypes, and we will create new layers for the new linetypes, so:

1 Still in AutoCAD with STDA3 drawing?

2 Ensure the screen is blank.

3 Make two new layers using the Layer Control dialogue box with:

layer name	linetype	colour	usage
L1	NEWLINE1	green	roads
L2	NEWLINE2	blue	shop outlines

4 When setting the linetypes to the new layers, the two newly created linetypes will be displayed in the Select Linetypes dialogue box.

5 Make two new text styles using:

Style name	text font
ST1	scriptc accepting all defaults
ST2	italict and accept ALL defaults.

6 Refer to Fig. 5.2 and produce a layout of your choice using:
a) NEWLINE1 (layer L1) for the roads
b) NEWLINE2 (layer L2) for the shops.

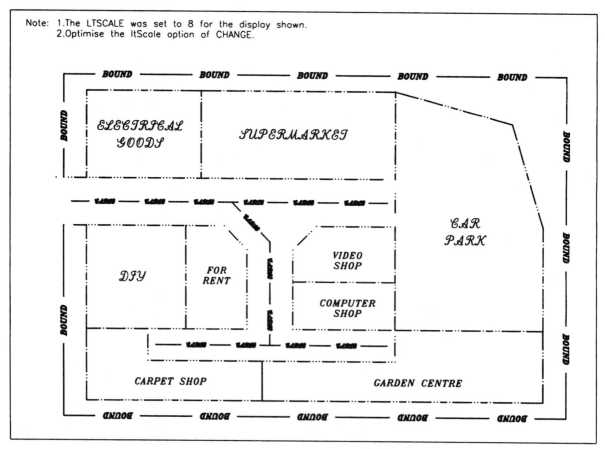

Figure 5.2 Shopping complex with two new (a) simple and (b) complex linetypes.

Note: my Fig. 5.2 displays other linetypes. Do not try to create or draw these yet.

7 Using your two new text styles, add names similar to those which are displayed.

8 Change your LTSCALE until you are satisfied with the linetype appearance.

9 When the drawing is complete, save the layout as **C:\R13CUST\SHOPLAY** as it will be used in other exercise.

10 Do not exit AutoCAD.

Linetype appearance

The appearance of non-continuous lines is controlled by LTSCALE and is global, i.e. all linetypes are redrawn to suit the new value of LTSCALE. It has not been possible with previous releases to display linetypes with different LTSCALE values at the one time. With R13 this can be obtained using the CHANGE or CHPROP commands. To demonstrate the effect we will use the two new linetypes so:

1 Erase your shopping area (after SAVE).

2 Set the LTSCALE to 12.

3 Draw a 200 length line with layer L1 current, and another with layer L2 current. Copy these two lines to three other parts of the screen.

4 At the command line enter **CHANGE** <R> and:

prompt	Select objects
respond	pick the first pair of drawn lines then right-click
prompt	Properties/<Change point>
enter	**P** <R> – the properties option
prompt	Change what properties (Color/Elev/LAyer/ltScale/Thicknss)
enter	**S** <R> – the ltscale option
prompt	New linetype scale<1>
enter	**0.5** <R>
prompt	Change what properties.....
respond	right-click.

5 The two lines will be displayed with a different appearance from the others.

6 Repeat the CHANGE command and select the third pair of lines and:

prompt	Properties..... and enter **P**
prompt	Change what..... and enter **S**
prompt	New linetype scale..... and enter **1.5**.

7 Finally use the P and S options of CHANGE and change the linetype scale of the fourth pair of lines to 2.

8 We now have four pairs of lines displayed at different scales. At the command line enter LTSCALE. Value is still 12?

9 *Note*. The ltScale option of the CHANGE (and CHPROP) command is new to Release 13. It allows individual linetypes to be scaled relative to the existing LTSCALE value and:
a) LTSCALE: 12, ltScale = 0.5 → effective LTSCALE 6
b) LTSCALE: 12, ltscale = 1.5 → effective LTSCALE 18.

10 The ltScale option was used to display the lines in Fig. 5.1.

11 This is a very useful addition to R13.

12 Do **not save** these changes.

Complex linetypes containing text

Release 13 allows linetypes to be created which contain items of text. We will discuss the complex linetypes already contained within AutoCAD and then create two new complex linetypes of our own.

1 Open your standard sheet and refer to Fig. 5.3.

2 At the command line enter **LINETYPE** <R> and:
prompt	?/Create... and enter **L** <R>
prompt	Linetype(s) to load and enter ***** <R>
prompt	Select Linetype File dialogue box
respond	*a*) check directory c:\r13\com\support
	b) pick file **ltypeshp.lin**
	c) pick OK
prompt	Linetype ???? loaded several times
then	?/Create...
respond	right-click

3 At the command line enter **SHELL** <R> and:
prompt	OS Command
enter	**EDIT C:\R13\COM\SUPPORT\LTYPESHP.LIN** <R>
prompt	Text editor
with	LTYPESHP AutoCAD Linetype file

4 Study the linetype descriptors displayed and note that they:
a) begin with *NAME, description
b) begin with A, in the second line
c) contain new items within **[ ]** brackets.

5 It is the addition of the items within the [ ] brackets which allows text to be added to linetypes. The linetype descriptors for this file are displayed in Fig. 5.3(a).

6 The format for complex linetypes is:

*NAME, description
A,pen movements,["TEXT",ST,S,R,X,Y]

7 The items contained within the [] are field definitions and determine how the item of text will be aligned relative to the line and:

"TEXT":	the actual text item contained within " ".
ST:	a text style which must be loaded into the drawing.
S:	the scale factor which will determine the text height in the line. This height is dependent on the text style height, the value of S and the LTSCALE value.
R:	the text rotation in the line.
X and Y:	are offsets for the text item computed from the end of the linetype definition vertex.

8 Figure 5.3(b) displays lines created using these complex linetypes and have been drawn with an LTSCALE of 12.

9 *Task.*
a) Create several new layers and set a different complex linetype to each new layer.
b) Draw several entities with each layer current.
c) Investigate the effect of LTSCALE and the ltScale option of the CHANGE command of these entities
d) Do not save this drawing.

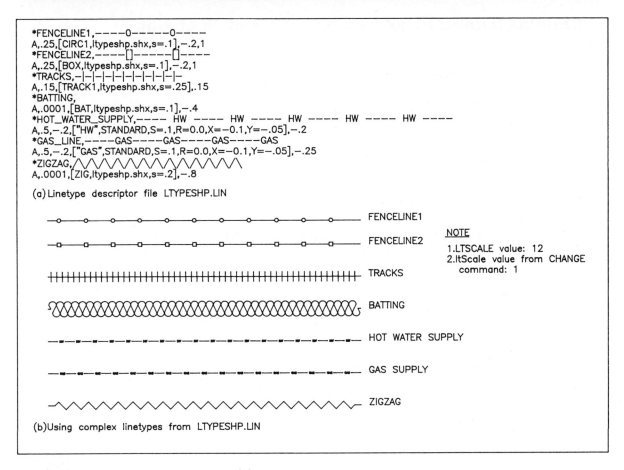

```
*FENCELINE1,————0—————0————
A,.25,[CIRC1,ltypeshp.shx,s=.1],—.2,1
*FENCELINE2,————[]—————[]————
A,.25,[BOX,ltypeshp.shx,s=.1],—.2,1
*TRACKS,—|—|—|—|—|—|—|—|—|—
A,.15,[TRACK1,ltypeshp.shx,s=.25],.15
*BATTING,
A,.0001,[BAT,ltypeshp.shx,s=.1],—.4
*HOT_WATER_SUPPLY,———— HW ———— HW ———— HW ———— HW ———— HW ————
A,.5,—.2,["HW",STANDARD,S=.1,R=0.0,X=—0.1,Y=—.05],—.2
*GAS_LINE,————GAS————GAS————GAS————GAS
A,.5,—.2,["GAS",STANDARD,S=.1,R=0.0,X=—0.1,Y=—.05],—.25
*ZIGZAG,/\/\/\/\/\/\/\/\/\/\
A,.0001,[ZIG,ltypeshp.shx,s=.2],—.8
```

(a) Linetype descriptor file LTYPESHP.LIN

FENCELINE1

FENCELINE2

TRACKS

BATTING

HOT WATER SUPPLY

GAS SUPPLY

ZIGZAG

NOTE
1. LTSCALE value: 12
2. ltScale value from CHANGE
   command: 1

(b) Using complex linetypes from LTYPESHP.LIN

Figure 5.3   Complex linetypes containing text.

Creating/loading/using two new complex linetypes

We will add the two new linetypes to our existing linetype file so:

1 Re-open drawing SHOPLAY.

2 Ensure text styles ST1 and ST2 have been created.

3 At the command line enter **SHELL** <R> and:

prompt	OS Command
enter	**EDIT C:\R13CUST\MYLINE.LIN** <R>
prompt	Text editor
with	two existing linetype descriptors
respond	cursor down below last line then enter:
	*CABLE, cable linetype <R>
	A,.5,−.25,["CABLE",ST1,S=.1,R=0,X=−0.1,Y=−0.05],−.5 <R>
	*BOUNDARY, boundary linetype <R>
	A,1,−.25,["BOUND",ST2,S=.1,R=0,X=−0.1,Y=−0.05],−.625 <R>

4 From the menu bar select File–Save As and:
  a) check directory C:\R13CUST
  b) check file name MYLINE.LIN
  c) pick OK

5 Select File–Exit from menu bar to return to drawing.

6 Load the two new linetypes with:
  a) LINETYPE <R>
  b) enter L <R> – load option
  c) enter * <R> – all linetypes
  d) pick C:\R13CUST directory
  e) pick MYLINE.LIN file
  f) enter Y <R> to any linetypes already loaded.

7 If there are no errors in your two new linetypes:
  prompt   Linetype CABLE loaded
         Linetype BOUNDARY loaded

8 Make two new layers:
  a) L3 with CABLE linetype
  b) L4 with BOUNDARY linetype

9 Making each new layer current, refer to Fig. 5.2 and add the cable and boundary lines.

10 Optimize the ltScale factor of the CHANGE (CHPROP) command until the linetypes are to your requirement.

11 Save the layout as SHOPLAY.

12 This completes the linetype exercise – except for the activity.

Summary

1 Linetypes can be:
  a) simple: dashes, dots and spaces
  b) complex: containing text items
2 The AutoCAD linetypes are contained in files:
  a) simple: ACAD.LIN
  b) complex: LTYPESHP.LIN
3 New linetypes can be created:
  a) from within AutoCAD with LINETYPE
  b) using a text editor, e.g. SHELL-EDIT
4 New linetypes can be stored:
  a) within the existing .lin files (not recommended)
  b) in new linetype files.
5 All linetypes consist of a two line **DESCRIPTOR** whose format is very strict and cannot be altered. It is:
  *NAME, description
  A,coded definitions
6 Complex linetypes contain field definitions within the coded part of the linetype descriptor. These field definitions determine how text will be aligned with the line and is:
  ["TEXT",ST,S,R,X,Y]
7 The procedure for creating new linetypes is:
  a) create the linetypes in a .LIN file
  b) load the linetypes
  c) set the linetypes in layers.
8 The appearance of linetypes is controlled by LTSCALE.
9 The ltScale option of CHANGE (and CHPROP) allows individual linetypes to be scaled relative to the current LTSCALE value.
10 New linetypes must be:
  a) created in a file
  b) loaded into the drawing
  c) set onto a layer.

Activity

The regional council which developed the shopping complex also decided to build a sports complex next to it, and it is the layout of the stadium which is the linetype activity.

Tutorial 4(a)

Using your STDA3 standard sheet and the linetype file MYLINE.LIN create:
a) the simple linetype SECTOR
b) the complex linetype TRACK

Tutorial 4(b)

Using the two newly created linetypes (as well as linetype BOUNDARY) completed the stadium layout. Alter the value of LTSCALE and ltScale to optimize the layout. When complete, save the layout as C:\R13CUST\STADIUM as it will be used for the activity on hatching. Remember to make new text styles, ST1 script and ST2 italict.

Chapter 6

Customizing hatch patterns

Hatch pattern customization is similar to linetype design but is more involved. The AutoCAD hatch patterns are all contained in the one file – **acad.pat** and new hatch patterns can be:

a) added to this file
b) created in separate hatch pattern files.

In our investigation into hatch patterns we will create new patterns in new files and leave the original hatch pattern file untouched.

What are hatch patterns?

Hatch patterns consist of combinations of straight lines and spaces, i.e. pen down and pen up movements, and must contain a minimum of two lines:

a) the header line
b) the pattern lines.

To view the AutoCAD hatch patterns:

1 Open the STDA3 standard sheet.

2 At the command line enter **SHELL** <R> and:
   prompt   OS Command
   enter   **EDIT C:\R13\COM\SUPPORT\ACAD.PAT** <R>
   prompt   MS DOS Editor with the AutoCAD hatch patterns
   respond scroll down the file and note two of the patterns are:
         a) ANGLE, Angle steel
            0, 0,0, 0,.275, .2,–.075
            90, 0,0, 0,.275, .2,–.075
         b) BRASS, Brass material
            0, 0,0, 0,.25
            0, 0,.125, 0,.25, .125,–.0625

3 Study other patterns and note that their 'complexity' is very varied.

4 Select File–Exit to return to the drawing screen.

Hatch pattern descriptors

Every hatch pattern consists of (at least) a two line **DESCRIPTOR** made up of three distinct parts:

1 The name of the hatch pattern preceded by an asterisk (*), e.g. *BRASS, *ANGLE. Capital letters are recommended for the name.

2 A written description of the hatch pattern. It follows the name and is *separated from it with a comma (,)*. The descriptive text is recommended as small letters.

3 The actual hatch pattern line(s) which are coded definitions of the hatch pattern. The format of these lines is:
   a) the ANGLE(ANG) from the horizontal
   b) the X ORIGIN (X) offset
   c) the Y ORIGIN (Y) offset
   d) the OFFSET DISPLACEMENT (OX) in the X direction
   e) the OFFSET DISPLACEMENT (OY) in the Y direction **PERPENDICULAR to the original pattern line**
   f) the pattern codes, i.e. pen down/up movements.

Note

1 The letters *a*)–*f*) will be referred to in our examples.

2 The hatch pattern name and descriptive text are always written as the first line, e.g. *BRASS, Brass material. This line is called the **HEADER** line.

3 The pen down/up movements are given as drawing units and one drawing unit is 1 mm.

4 There must be at least one pattern code line.

5 A maximum of six dashed lengths are permitted in a pattern line.

6 The format of the hatch pattern descriptor is very strict and cannot be altered. It is:

*NAME, description
ANG, X,Y, OX,OY, pen movements

First pattern line for discussion

The first hatch pattern we will investigate in detail is:

```
*BRASS, Brass material      – header line
0, 0,0, 0,.25              – pattern line 1
0, 0,.125, 0,.25, .125,–.0625  – pattern line 2
```

The hatch pattern is detailed in Fig. 6.1 and displays:
a) the hatch pattern descriptor
b) the hatch pattern construction and sizes as drawing units
c) using the hatch pattern at different scales and angles.

1 Header line: name of pattern   *BRASS
                        description   Brass material

2 Pattern line 1: 0, 0,0, 0,.25 – ref a), b), c), d), e):
   a) 0 angle, i.e. a horizontal line – original pattern line 1
   b) 0 X origin offset
   c) 0 Y origin offset, i.e. pattern line 1 origin is at an assumed point (0,0)
   d) 0 X offset displacement, i.e. no horizontal displacement between successive lines of this type
   e) .25 Y offset displacement, i.e. there is .25 drawing units vertical displacement PERPENDICULAR to the original pattern line 1 between successive lines of this type
   f) no pen down/up movements given which means that a continuous line will be drawn.

3 Pattern line 2: 0, 0,.125, 0,.25, .125,–.0625 – a), b), c), d), e), f):
   a) 0 angle, i.e. another horizontal line – original pattern line 2
   b) 0 X origin offset
   c) .125 Y origin offset, i.e. there is a vertical offset of .125 drawing units from the (0,0) assumed origin point. Pattern line 2 has its origin at the point (0,.125) relative to pattern line 1
   d) 0 X offset displacement, i.e. no horizontal displacement between successive lines of this type
   e) .25 Y offset displacement, i.e. there is .25 drawing units vertical displacement PERPENDICULAR to the original pattern line 2 between successive lines of this type
   f) .125 and –.0625 are the pen movements, i.e. pen down for .125 drawing units then pen up for .0625 drawing units. This will be repeated until the hatch boundary is reached.

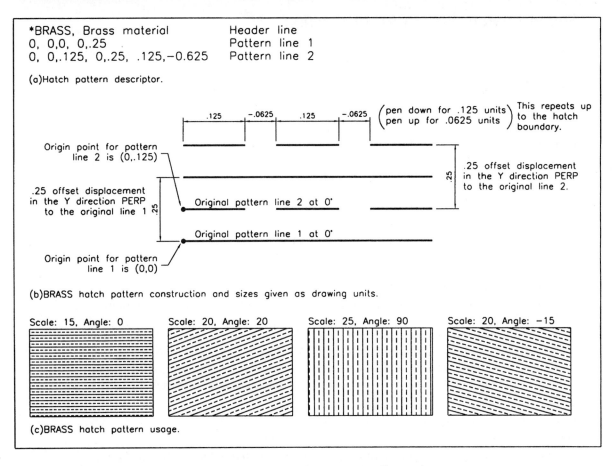

```
*BRASS, Brass material          Header line
0, 0,0, 0,.25                   Pattern line 1
0, 0,.125, 0,.25, .125,−0.625   Pattern line 2
```

(a)Hatch pattern descriptor.

(b)BRASS hatch pattern construction and sizes given as drawing units.

(c)BRASS hatch pattern usage.

Figure 6.1 Details of brass hatch pattern – descriptor, construction and usage.

Second hatch pattern for discussion

This hatch pattern is:

*ANGLE, Angle steel	– header line
0, 0,0, 0,.275, .2,–.075	– pattern line 1
90, 0,0, 0,.275, .2,–.075	– pattern line 2

The hatch pattern is detailed in Fig. 6.2 with:
a) the hatch pattern descriptor
b) the pattern construction with sizes as drawing units
c) using the pattern at different scales and angles.

1 Header line: name of pattern   *ANGLE
               description   Angle steel

2 Pattern line 1: 0, 0,0, 0,.275, .2,–.075 – *a*), *b*), *c*), *d*), *e*), *f*):
a) 0 angle, i.e. a horizontal line – original pattern line 1
b) 0 X origin offset
c) 0 Y origin offset, i.e. pattern line 1 starts at an assumed point (0,0)
d) 0 X offset displacement, i.e. no horizontal displacement between successive lines of this type
e) .275 Y offset displacement, i.e. there is .275 drawing units vertical displacement PERPENDICULAR to the original pattern line 1 between successive lines of this type
f) .2 and –.075 are the pen movements, i.e. pen down for .2 drawing units then pen up for .075 drawing units. This will repeat until the hatch boundary is reached.

3 Pattern line 2: 90, 0,0, 0,.275, .2,–.075 – *a*), *b*), *c*), *d*), *e*), *f*):
a) 90 angle, i.e. a vertical line – original pattern line 2
b) 0 X origin offset
c) 0 Y origin offset, i.e. the origin point for pattern line 2 is (0,0) which is the same origin point for pattern line 1. Thus pattern lines 1 and 2 both start at the same assumed point
d) 0 X offset displacement, i.e. no horizontal displacement between successive lines of this type
e) .275 Y offset displacement, i.e. there is .275 drawing units vertical displacement PERPENDICULAR to the original pattern line 2 between successive lines of this type
f) .2 and –.075 are the pen movements, i.e. pen down for .2 drawing units then pen up for .075 drawing units. This will repeat until the hatch boundary is reached.

Note

Probably the most difficult and confusing concept in hatch pattern customization is the *X* and *Y* offset displacement – at least it was for me. Hopefully this note will remove any confusion.

a) The X offset displacement is in the direction of the original pattern line.
b) The Y offset displacement is **ALWAYS PERPENDICULAR to the original pattern line**.

Thus if the original pattern line is at 90 degrees, i.e. vertical:

a) the *X* offset displacement is in the traditional *y* direction
b) the *Y* offset displacement is in the traditional *x* direction.

Refer to pattern line 1 and 2 in Fig. 6.2 and you will realise that it is relatively straightforward. The phrase PERPENDICULAR to the original pattern line is important.

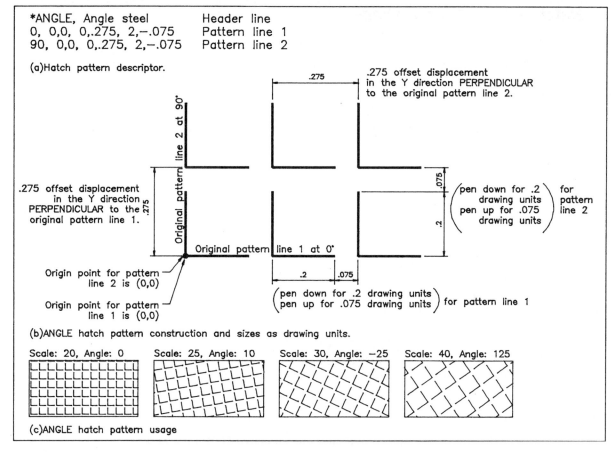

Figure 6.2 Details of ANGLE hatch pattern – decription, construction and usage.

Designing our own hatch patterns

As stated earlier, new hatch patterns can be created:

a) within the existing acad.pat file
b) in user-defined .pat files.

At this stage we will create our own hatch pattern files in our R13CUST directory. When new hatch pattern files are being created:

1 only one pattern can be stored in the file
2 the file must have the same name as the hatch pattern being created.

We will create four new hatch patterns, these being:

1 a T pattern
2 a double square pattern
3 a weave pattern
4 an arrow pattern.

Note: when I design hatch patterns I try to work with a basic shape which contains one complete element of the pattern. This shape is usually rectangular as it allows for easy 'tiling'.

Hatch pattern 1 – tee shapes

This pattern is fairly simple and consists of three lines.

1 Open your STDA3 standard sheet and refer to Fig. 6.3 which displays the following information about the pattern to be created:
- *a*) the basic element sizes as drawing units
- *b*) six basic repeating elements and the three line pattern identification
- *c*) the three line origin points relative to an assumed 0,0 pattern origin
- *d*) the three line descriptors
- *e*) using the hatch pattern at different scales and angles.

2 At the command line enter **SHELL** <R> and:

prompt	OS Command
enter	**EDIT C:\R13CUST\TSHAPE.PAT** <R>
prompt	MS DOS text editor
respond	*a*) enter the following:

        *TSHAPE, tee shapes <R>
        0, 0,5, 0,6, 5,–1 <R>
        90, 3,0, 0,6, 5,–1 <R>
        90, 5,5, 0,6, 1,–5 <R>

    b) pick File–Save As and:
      i)   check directory is C:\R13CUST
      ii)   check file name is TSHAPE.PAT
      iii) pick OK
    c) pick File–Exit to return to drawing screen.

3 With layer OUT current draw some simple shapes for hatching.

4 Make layer SECT current and at the command line enter **HATCH** <R> and:

prompt	Pattern.....
enter	**TSHAPE** <R>
prompt	Scale for Pattern and enter **2** <R>
prompt	Angle for Pattern and enter **0** <R>
prompt	Select objects
respond	window a shape then right-click

5 If the TSHAPE pattern was created correctly, hatching will be added to the selected shape.

6 Select the Hatch icon and:

prompt	Boundary Hatch dialogue box
with	*a*) Pattern type: Custom
	b) Custom Pattern: TSHAPE
respond	*i*) alter scale to 3
	ii) alter angle to 20
	iii) pick Pick Points and pick an internal point within one of your shapes
	iv) Preview–Continue–Apply

7 Hatch the other shapes, altering the scale and angle values.

8 *Hatch errors.*

There are two main errors which may be encountered when creating hatch patterns, these being:

a) The 'bad definition' error message. This usually results when a period (.) is used instead of a comma (,) and requires the hatch pattern file to be altered.

b) The hatching seems to take some time to fill the shape. This usually means that the line descriptors are wrong, or that the scale factor is too low. Press **ESC** to cancel the command and check the descriptors or increase the scale value.

9 Continue to the next exercise. Save is not required.

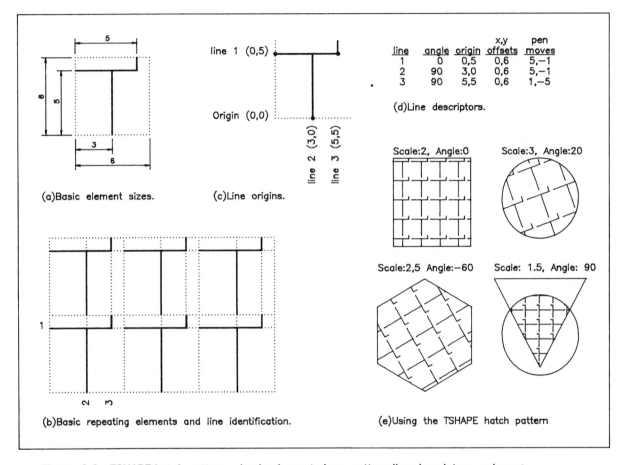

Figure 6.3 TSHAPE hatch pattern – basic element sizes, pattern line descriptors and usage.

Hatch pattern 2 – double squares

This pattern is slightly more difficult than the first exercise. It consists of two squares and requires eight lines to be created.

1 Open the STDA3 standard sheet and refer to Fig. 6.4 which displays:
   a) the basic element sizes as drawing units
   b) four repeating elements in the pattern
   c) the eight line origins
   d) the line descriptors
   e) different pattern usage.

2 At the command line enter **SHELL** <R> then:
   EDIT C:\R13CUST\DOUBLE.PAT
   *DOUBLE, double square
   0, 0,0, 0,8, 6,–2
   0, 2,2, 0,8, 2,–6
   0, 2,4, 0,8, 2,–6
   0, 0,6, 0,8, 6,–2
   90, 0,0, 0,8, 6,–2
   90, 2,2, 0,8, 2,–6
   90, 4,2, 0,8, 2,–6
   90, 6,0, 0,8, 6,–2

3 File–Save As–OK then File–Exit.

4 Draw some shapes then select the Hatch icon to display the Boundary Hatch dialogue box and:
   a) Pattern Type: pick **Custom**
   b) Custom Pattern: enter **DOUBLE**
   c) Scale: enter **2**
   d) Angle: enter **0**
   e) Pick **Points**: pick an internal point in one of the shapes
   f) Preview–Continue–Apply.

5 Hatch the other shapes, altering the scale and angle values.

6 Do not save, but continue to the next exercise.

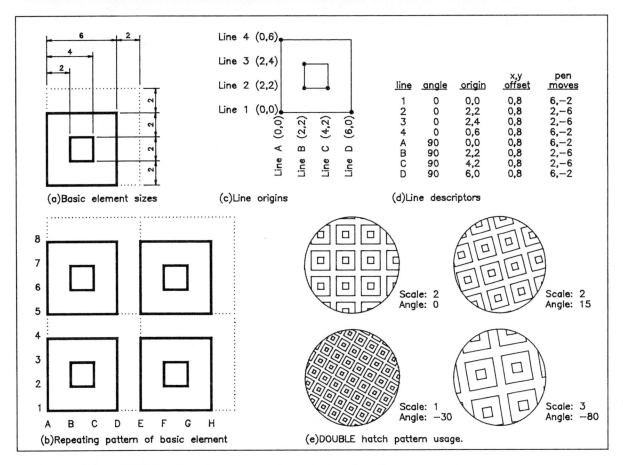

(a)Basic element sizes

(c)Line origins

(d)Line descriptors

line	angle	origin	x,y offset	pen moves
1	0	0,0	0,8	6,−2
2	0	2,2	0,8	2,−6
3	0	2,4	0,8	2,−6
4	0	0,6	0,8	6,−2
A	90	0,0	0,8	6,−2
B	90	2,2	0,8	2,−6
C	90	4,2	0,8	2,−6
D	90	6,0	0,8	6,−2

(b)Repeating pattern of basic element

Scale: 2
Angle: 0

Scale: 2
Angle: 15

Scale: 1
Angle: −30

Scale: 3
Angle: −80

(e)DOUBLE hatch pattern usage.

Figure 6.4 DOUBLE hatch pattern – basic element sizes, line descriptors and usage.

Hatch pattern 3 – a weave pattern

This is a complex pattern made from four horizontal and four vertical lines and is detailed in Fig. 6.5. with:

a) the basic element sizes
b) repeating elements in the pattern
c) the eight line origin points
d) the line descriptors
e) the pattern usage at different scales and angles.

The pattern is created by line 1 being repeated at line 5, line 2 at line 6, line A at line E, etc. All offsets are 6 due to the pattern being square. The complete pattern is created with:

```
SHELL
EDIT C:\R13CUST\WEAVE.PAT
*WEAVE, a weave pattern effect
0, 0,0, 0,6, 4.5,−1.5
0, 0,1.5, 0,6, 1.5,−1.5,3
0, 0,3, 0,6, 1.5,−1.5,3
0, 0,4.5, 0,6, 4.5,−1.5
90, 0,0, 0,6, 1.5,−1.5,3
90, 1.5,0, 0,6, 4.5,−1.5
90, 3,0, 0,6, 4.5,−1.5
90, 4.5,0, 0,6, 1.5,−1.5,3
File–Save As OK
File–Exit
```

Use the pattern to add hatching to some shapes.

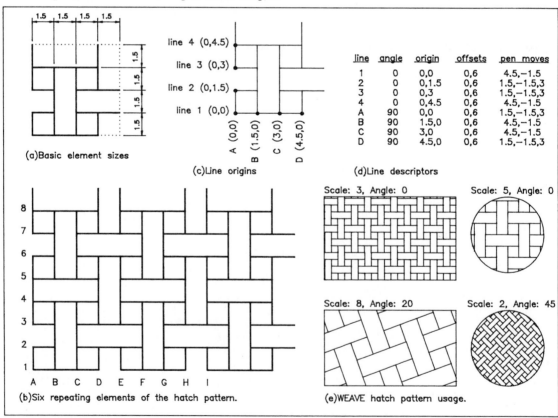

Figure 6.5 WEAVE hatch pattern – basic element, line descriptors and usage.

Hatch pattern 4 – an arrow pattern *(compliments of Bob McNay)*

This pattern only contains four lines but is very complex as it contains 'angled' lines. When hatch patterns have lines which are not horizontal or vertical, the offsets usually require the use of trig. to obtain the actual offset distance values. My actual arrow shape was a basic 3,4,5 triangle, selected to make the pen up/down movements easy. The angles associated with these values are 36.8699 and 143.1301. You can check the offset values or simply accept my values. To create this hatch pattern:

1 Open your standard sheet and refer to Fig. 6.6 which details:
   a) the basic arrow shape sizes
   b) repeating elements of the pattern with the offset distances displayed and evaluated. This diagram is rather 'cluttered' as I used it to portray all the offsets at once
   c) the line origins relative to a selected (0,0) origin point
   d) using the created pattern.

2 If you are unsure of the offsets, draw the pattern to scale and measure the offset distances.

3 At the command line enter **SHELL** <R> and then the following lines:
   EDIT C:\R13CUST\ARROW.PAT
   *ARROW, arrow type pattern
   0, 0,5, 16,12, 8,–24
   36.8699, 0,5, 14.4,19.2, 5,–15
   90, 4,0, 12,16, 8,–16
   143.1301, 8,5, 5.6,19.2, 5,–15

4 File–Save As then File–Exit as usual.

5 Use the hatch pattern but watch the scale value.

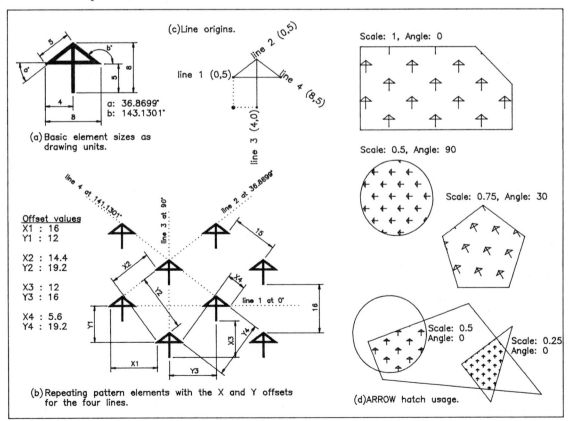

Figure 6.6 ARROW hatch pattern details.

Note

1 When the HATCH command is used, AutoCAD searches through .PAT files for the specified pattern name. The order of this search is:
a) the ACAD.PAT file in the SUPPORT sub-directory
b) other .PAT files in the working directory
c) the floppy drive.

2 It is recommended that hatch pattern files are created within the directory from which the drawing is being loaded.

Summary

1 All AutoCAD's hatch pattern files are contained in the file ACAD.PAT which is in the sub-directory SUPPORT.
2 All hatch patterns consist of a series of parallel lines.
3 The format for creating hatch patterns is very rigid and cannot be altered. This format is:
*NAME, description
angle, origin, offsets, pen movements
4 Customized hatch patterns can be created:
a) in the existing ACAD.PAT file
b) in new .PAT files.
5 New hatch pattern files **must have the same file name as the pattern**.
6 I recommend that new hatch patterns are created in new files.
7 The Y offset is probably the most difficult of the hatch concepts to understand. It should be remembered that this offset is always PERPENDICULAR to the direction of the original pattern line, no matter if this line is horizontal, vertical or inclined.
8 Hatch patterns are not affected by the LTSCALE command. It is the pattern scale factor which determines the hatch appearance.
9 Always start new hatching with a large scale factor and 'work downwards' until you obtain the optimum effect.

Activity

Two activities have been included for hatch patterns. The first activity simply involves using the newly created hatch patterns in an existing drawing. The second requires you to create a new pattern.

Tutorial 5

Use the STADIUM drawing from the linetype chapter and add the four created patterns. Use your imagination for the actual layout.

Tutorial 6

This is a new hatch pattern for customization, and the following information is given for you:

a) the basic element with sizes
b) the repeated pattern with the X and Y offset sizes
c) the pattern usage.

Create the pattern in a new file ARRHEAD in your R13CUST directory. I have given the offsets, but you will need to work out the pen movements for yourself.

Note: I found that moving and rotating the UCS helpful.

Chapter 7

Shapes

When a drawing element is to be used several times, the simplest way of achieving this is usually by creating and inserting a block. It may be necessary to insert the block repeatedly, e.g. when drawing an electronic/pneumatic circuit and the short delay experienced when inserting the block becomes noticeable and can slow down the draughting process, To overcome this SHAPES are used.

What are shapes?

Shapes are similar to blocks. They are drawing entities stored in the same way that AutoCAD stores its text fonts. The method of defining a shape is very concise and efficient, but it is not to as easy to create a shape as it is to make a block.

Despite any similarity in use, shapes and blocks have basic differences in the way they are defined. Blocks are a collection of drawn entities that are joined together to form a single entity. They are produced using straightforward drawing techniques and are saved either as part of the drawing file in which they are created (BLOCKS), or as separate drawings (WBLOCKS) which are available for use by other operators. Whole drawings can be inserted into other drawings as wblocks. The use of blocks saves memory in comparison to multiple copying of items. Blocks also have the added capacity of attributes, making the text information contained in a block available for extraction for use in other software packages.

Shapes are made from lines and arcs and are very suitable for items such as electrical symbols, alphabets, etc. Shapes are created within their own files which have the extension **.SHP** and are written using any text editor. The shape files can be stored in a named directory or on floppy disc. The AutoCAD text font files are created from shapes.

The process of defining shapes requires the very formal specification of a number of parameters. Shape definitions appear to be similar to linetype and hatch pattern descriptors but whereas linetypes and hatch patterns are written in a format suitable to a plotter (i.e. pen up and down movements), shapes are written as **screen vectors** in hexadecimal code.

Screen vectors: instructions stored in memory to position lines and circles on the screen. Hexadecimal: is a number system with a base of 16 and is the standard computer numbering system and:

Base 10:   0, 1, 2, 3, 4, 5, 6, 7, 8, 9, 10, 11, 12, 13, 14, 15
Hex equivalent: 0, 1, 2, 3, 4, 5, 6, 7, 8, 9, A, B, C, D, E, F

Computers use hexadecimal numbers from '00' to 'FF', i.e. 0 to 255. The memory space which stores these pairs of digits (the 00–FF) is called a **byte** and each byte is divided into two **nibbles**.

Shape descriptors

Every shape in a file must have its own unique two line definition and the format is:

*shapenumber, number of bytes, SHAPENAME
coded description of shape

a) The shapenumber is between 1 and 255 in any one file and *must be preceded by an asterisk (*)*, e.g. *4, *14, *144.

Note: the AutoCAD Manual specifies shapenumbers between 1 and 258 although numbers 256–258 are for special use.

b) Number of bytes: this is the total number of bytes in the actual shape definition. It is obtained by adding the bytes in the coded description line. A maximum of 2000 bytes is permitted per shape.

c) SHAPENAME: is the name used to recall the shape when it is to be used in a drawing. It must be in **CAPITAL LETTERS**, e.g. ARROW, RES.

d) Coded description: is a series of codes which relate to the vector direction and length, as well as other specialist codes.

e) A typical shape definition could be:
   *18,7,LSHP
   050,02C,020,03C,078,054,0

   i) 18 is the shape number in the file, preceded by *
   ii) 7 is the number of bytes in the description line
   iii) LSHP is the shape name in capitals
   iv) 050,02C, etc. are the coded descriptions of the vectors which make up the shape.
      Note: **1** the coded description line is usually written first to obtain the number of bytes which make up the shape.
      2 all hexadecimal letters in the coded descriptions must be in CAPITALS
      3 every line descriptor ends with a 0.

Predefined vector directions

There are 16 predefined vector directions available when drawing simple straight line elements in a shape. These are shown in Fig. 7.1.

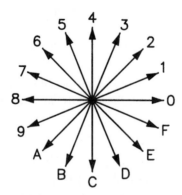

Figure 7.1 Predefined vector directions.

As an example of how predefined vectors are used, a vertical line drawn from bottom to top of length 5 units would be coded as **054**. If the line were drawn from top to bottom, the code would be **05C**.

Vector directions are always defined in a *three-digit format* as follows:

05C   0: the leading 0, signifying a hexadecimal number to follow

           5: the *length* of the vector

           C: the *direction* of the vector

Figure 7.2 displays the LSHP shape previously defined.

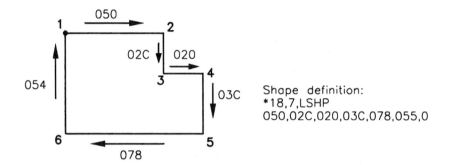

Figure 7.2   Shape definition example. Shape drawn from 1–2–3–4–5–6–1.

Note: **1** All shape definitions end with a 0.
               2 The end of definition 0 is included in the byte count.
               3 Byte line 2 should be completed before line 1.
               4 All sizes refer to drawing units, i.e. 1 mm.

Shape definition codes

Predefined vector directions can only be used if a straight line is to be created in one of the 16 predefined directions. Lines which are not in a predefined direction, arcs and circles can be created in a shape, but require a special shape definition code. There are several shape definition codes, but we will only investigate the most commonly used codes. Readers are referred to the AutoCAD Customization Guide which details in full all codes available.

The most common codes are:

000   *end* of shape definition (shortened to 0)
001   activates the draw mode, i.e. *pen down* (1 is acceptable)
002   de-activates the draw mode, i.e. *pen up*
003   *divide vector length* by next byte
004   *multiply vector length* by next byte
008   *X,Y displacement* given by next 2 bytes, e.g. (4,3)
009   *multiple X,Y displacements* terminated by (0,0)
00A   *octant arc* defined by next 5 bytes
            This code is usually written as 10
00B   *fractional arc* defined by next 5 bytes.

Some of these codes are worth a more detailed explanation:

003,004: enables vectors to be scaled when the SHAPE command is activated. The actual shape is made larger or smaller by the factor indicated in the byte following the code. These codes can be written as 3 or 4.

008: enables pen movement that is not possible with the predefined vectors, e.g. a movement of 6 units to the right and 1 unit downwards cannot be obtained by predefined vectors. Using the 008 (or 8) code, the required movement can be defined as **8,(6,–1)**. The brackets are not essential but I find them useful when the code has to be interpreted.
The code 8,(6,–1) has 3 bytes in it.
The convention for positive and negative movement is:

> left and down is negative
> right and up is positive.

Figure 7.3 displays a shape using the 008 code.

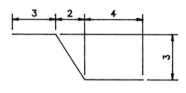

Shape description:
*19,6,SH1
030,8,(2,–3),040,0

Figure 7.3   008 Definition code example.

009: this is similar to the 008 code but is used when a sequence of non-standard vector movement is required, e.g. a movement of 7 right and 1 down followed by 6 left and 5 up would be coded as **9,(7,–1),(–6,5),(0,0)**. The 009 (or 9) code *is always terminated with (0,0)*. The code defined has 7 bytes in it.

Figure 7.4 displays a complete shape definition using the 009 code.

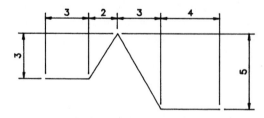

Shape description:
*20,10,SH2
030,9,(2,3),(3,–5),(0,0),040,0

Figure 7.4   009 Definition code example.

00A: enables **octantarcs** (i.e. 1/8th of a circle) to be drawn. Fig. 7.4 displays the octant arc numbers and the format for using the code is:

10,R,(+ or −)0ST

10:	the octant arc code, used instead of 00A
R:	radius of arc
+:	arc drawn in an anti-clockwise direction
−:	arc drawn in a clockwise direction
0:	leading 0 for hexadecimal
S:	number of the starting octant
T:	number of octants spanned by the arc.

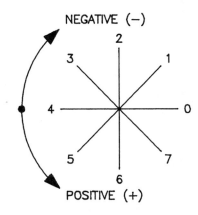

Figure 7.5 Octant arc number system with directions.

A shape using the code **10,5,+043** (Fig. 7.6) can be interpreted as:

10:	the octant arc code (used instead of 00A)
5:	arc radius is 5
+:	arc to be drawn in an anticlockwise direction
0:	leading 0 for hexadecimal
4:	starting octant arc quadrant
3:	arc drawn through three octant quadrants

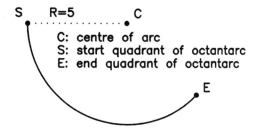

Figure 7.6 Octant arc example.

Creating three shapes

We will now create three shapes and discuss how the shape definition is constructed for each. The shapes will be displayed in detail with drawing unit sizes given.

Shape 1: a cross, using the codes 1 and 2

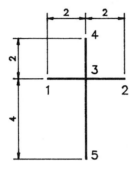

The shape has been drawn:
1 from 1 to 2 with pen down, i.e. 1,040
2 from 2 to 3 then 3 to 4 with pen up, i.e. 2,028,024
3 from 4 to 5 with pen down, i.e. 1,06C

The complete definition is:
    *11,8,CROSS
    1,040,2,028,024,1,06C,0

Note.
a) 11 is an arbitrary shape number.
b) The coded definition ends with 0.
c) I would probably have written the second line as:
    040,028,024,06C,0 – why?

Shape 2: a quadrant which uses code 00A (or 10)

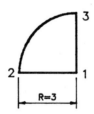

This shape is drawn:
1 as a line from 1 to 2, i.e. 038
2 as an octant from 2 to 3, i.e. 10,3,–042
3 as a line from 3 to 1, i.e. 03C

The complete definition for this shape is:
*12,6,QUAD
038,10,3,–042,03C,0

Shape 3: a tab which requires the multiple sequence 9 code

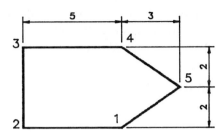

The shape has been drawn as lines:
1 from 1 to 2, i.e. 058
2 from 2 to 3, i.e. 044
3 from 3 to 4, i.e. 050
4 from 4 to 5 to 1, i.e. 9,(3,–2),(–3,–2),(0,0).

The complete shape definition is:
*13,11,TAB
058,044,050,9,(3,–2),(–3,–2),(0,0),0

Writing a shape file

Once the shape definitions have been obtained, it is necessary to write a shape file for them before they can be used in a drawing. As shape files are text files (with the extension .SHP) they are written with a text editor, so:

1 Open your STDA3 standard sheet and display the Miscellaneous toolbar.

2 At the command line enter **SHELL** <R> and:
prompt	OS Command
enter	**EDIT :\R13CUST\MYSHAPE.SHP** <R>
prompt	MS DOS text editor screen
respond	enter the following lines:
	*11,8,CROSS
	1,040,2,028,024,1,06C,0
	*12,6,QUAD
	038,10,3,–042,03C,0
	*13,11,TAB
	058,044,050,9,(3,–2),(–3,–2),(0,0),0
then	select File–Save As and:
	a) check directory is C:\R13CUST
	b) check file name is MYSHAPE.SHP
	c) pick OK
then	select File–Exit to return to drawing screen.

Compiling a shape file

The file which has just been written cannot be used by AutoCAD to draw shapes. This is because AutoCAD does not work with .SHP files. Shape files must be *compiled* before the shapes they contain can be used. Compiled shape files have the extension **.SHX**. To compile the file containing the three shapes:

1 From the menu bar select **Tools–Compile...** and:
prompt   Select Shape or Font File dialogue box
respond   *a*) change directory to **C:\R13CUST**
       b) pick **myshape.shp**
       c) pick OK
prompt   Compiling shape/font description file
       Compilation successful
       Output file C:\R13CUST\MYSHAPE.shx contains 85 bytes.

2 It is possible that the compilation will not be successful. This is usually because the user has made a mistake when writing the original .SHP file. The most common errors are:
a) not having the correct number of bytes in the second line
b) not using capital letters for the shape name
c) using the letter O instead of the number 0
d) not using the leading 0 in vector definitions, i.e. 58 instead of 058
e) not using capital letters in the definition, i.e. 06a instead of 06A
f) forgetting to end the shape definition with 0.

3 If there is an error, AutoCAD will prompt with a message similar to one of the following:
a) Bad shape definition at line xx of C:_____.shp
b) Invalid shape element or bad syntax.

Using shapes

When a shape file has been compiled it must be loaded into AutoCAD before the shapes can be used. You should still have your STDA3 standard sheet opened, so:

1 From the menu bar select **Data**
                                Shape File...
prompt   Select Shape File dialogue box
respond   *a*) directory c:\r13cust
       b) pick **myshape.shx** – note extension
       c) pick OK
prompt   Command line returned.

2 Select the Shape icon from the Miscellaneous toolbar and:
prompt   Shape name (or ?)
enter   **?** <R>
prompt   Shape(s) to list <*>
respond   right-click
prompt   Text screen with
       File: MYSHAPE.SHX
            CROSS   QUAD
            TAB
respond   F2 to flip back to drawing screen.

3 Select the shape icon again and:
prompt   Shape name (or ?)
enter   **CROSS** <R>
prompt   Starting point and enter **20,250** <R>
prompt   Height and enter **1** <R>
prompt   Rotation angle and enter **0** <R>.

4 The cross shape (quite small?) will be displayed at the entered point.

5 At the command line enter **SHAPE** <R> and:
prompt   Shape name (or ?)<CROSS>
enter   **QUAD** <R>
prompt   Starting point and enter **70,250** <R>
prompt   Height<1> and right-click
prompt   Rotation angle<0> and right-click.

6 Repeat the shape command with:
shape name: **TAB**
starting point: **120,250**
height: **1**
rotation: **0**.

7 Refer to Fig. 7.7(A) and use the shape command (icon or command line) to 'insert' the three shapes at different heights and rotation angles.

8 Save the drawing at this stage.

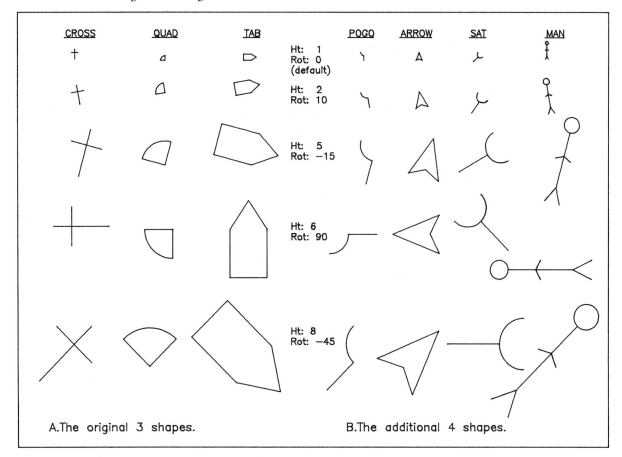

Figure 7.7 The shapes from the MYSHAPE.SHP file.

Another four shapes

Defining shapes requires patience and practice and I have included four shapes to add to our shape file. The complete shape definition is given with the figures which follow.

1 The first extra shape consist of a circle quadrant with a line attached at one end.

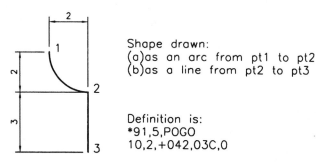

Shape drawn:
(a)as an arc from pt1 to pt2
(b)as a line from pt2 to pt3

Definition is:
*91,5,POGO
10,2,+042,03C,0

*91:   the shape number in the MYSHAPE.SHP file
5:         the number of bytes in the coded definitions
POGO: the name of the shape
10:        code for an octant arc
2:         arc radius of 2 units
+042:   counter-clockwise (+) arc starting at octant 4 and drawn through 2 octants
03C: straight line 3 units vertically downwards from the last point which is the endpoint of the octant arc
0:         end of shape definition.

2 This shape is an arrow head which is drawn with multiple *X, Y* displacements.

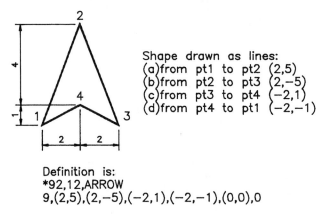

Shape drawn as lines:
(a)from pt1 to pt2 (2,5)
(b)from pt2 to pt3 (2,−5)
(c)from pt3 to pt4 (−2,1)
(d)from pt4 to pt1 (−2,−1)

Definition is:
*92,12,ARROW
9,(2,5),(2,−5),(−2,1),(−2,−1),(0,0),0

The 009 code is used to draw the necessary lines. The shape definition ends with (0,0),0
i.e.
(0,0):   end of 009 code
0:         end of shape definition.

3 The third shape is a type of satellite dish, and hopefully the shape definition is relatively easy for you to interpret.

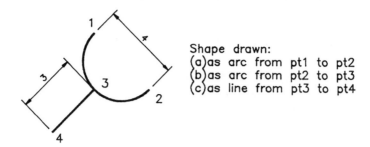

Shape drawn:
(a) as arc from pt1 to pt2
(b) as arc from pt2 to pt3
(c) as line from pt3 to pt4

Definition is:
*93,8,SAT
10,2,+034,10,2,−072,03A,0

4 The last additional shape is the 'thin man' and requires a circle for the head, obtained using the octant arc (10) code.

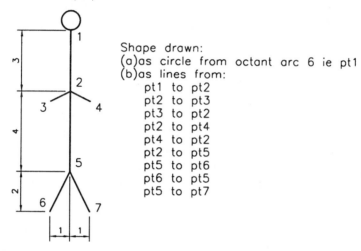

Shape drawn:
(a) as circle from octant arc 6 ie pt1
(b) as lines from:
    pt1 to pt2
    pt2 to pt3
    pt3 to pt2
    pt2 to pt4
    pt4 to pt2
    pt2 to pt5
    pt5 to pt6
    pt6 to pt5
    pt5 to pt7

Definition is:
*94,19,MAN
10,1,060,03C,019,011,01F,017,04C,9,(−1,−2),(1,2),(1,−2),(0,0),0

10,1,060: octant arc code is 10
      radius of circle is 1
      octant arc starts at octant 6
      circle effect with 0.

Using the additional four shapes

The four new shapes must be added to the existing shape file, so:

1 Open the drawing saved earlier of the three original shapes.

2 At the command line enter **SHELL** <R> and:

prompt   OS Command
enter   **EDIT C:\R13CUST\MYSHAPE.SHP** <R>
prompt   MS DOS Editor with the six original shape lines
respond   *a*) scroll to below the last line
        b) enter the following:
           *91,5,POGO
           10,2,+042,03C,0
           *92,12,ARROW
           9,(2,5),(2,−5),(−2,1),(−2,−1),(0,0),0
           *93,8,SAT
           10,2,+034,10,2,−072,03A,0
           *94,19,MAN
           10,1,060,03C,019,011,01F,017,04C,9,(−1,−2),(1,2),(1,−2),(0,0),0
      c) pick File–Save As from the menu bar
      d) pick File–Exit to return to drawing screen.

3 The new shape file must be re-compiled and loaded so:
    a) select Tools–Compile... and pick myshape.shp
    b) select Data–Shape File... and pick myshape.shx

4 Refer to Fig. 7.7(B) and add the four new shapes at different heights and rotation angles. *Note*: When an existing .SHP file is modified then re-compiled and loaded, you may find that the modification 'does not work'. I would recommend that when you alter a shape file you then re-open the drawing and then use the SHAPE command.

AutoCAD's shape files

AutoCAD R13 has three shape files supplied with it. To find out if these files have been installed in your system open your standard sheet and:

1 Enter **FILES** <R> at the command line to display the File Utilities dialogue box

2 Pick List files... to display the File List dialogue box.

3 *a*) select the C:\R13\COM directory
    b) select the sample sub-directory
    c) change File name to ***.shp**
    d) list is es.shp; pc.shp; st.shp
    e) Cancel the File list dialogue box
    f) Exit the File Utilities dialogue box.

4 If the three shape files are installed in your system they can be used for:
    a) es.shp – electrical circuit symbols
    b) pc.shp – printed circuit symbols
    c) st.shp – surface texture symbols.

5 The shape files must be compiled so select Tools–Compile... and:
    a) change directory to **c:\r13\com\sample**
    b) alter file name to ***.shp**
    c) pick the file **es.shp**
    d) pick OK.

6 Load the es,shp file with Data–Shape File... and:
   a) directory **c;\r13\com\sample**
   b) pick **es.shx** then OK.

7 Before the shapes from the file can be used it is necessary to know the shape names, so select the Shape icon and:
   prompt   Shape name (or ?) and enter ? <R>
   prompt   Shape to list and enter * <R>
   prompt   Text screen with:
              C:\R13\COM\SAMPLE\ES.SHX
              CON1   RES
              CAP   DIODE
              PNP   NPN
              MARK   ARROW
              JUMP   CON2
              ZENER   OR
              NOR   XOR
              AND   NAND
              BUFFER   INVERTER
              BOX   NEG
   respond F2 to flip back to drawing screen.

8 Refer to Fig. 7.8 which displays all the shapes from the ES.SHP file at heights of 25 or 15.

9 *Task*. Compile–Load–Use the shapes from the PC.SHP and ST.SHP files using Fig. 7.8 as a reference. Remember that you will need to list the shapes to obtain the shape names (step 7 above).

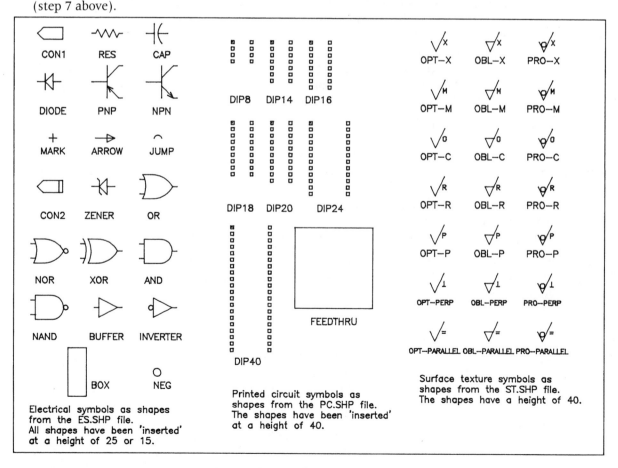

Figure 7.8 Symbols from AutoCAD's three shape files.

Complex linetypes containing shapes

In Chapter 5 linetypes were created which contained text items. It was also mentioned that complex linetypes could be customized to contain shapes. In this section we will investigate how complex linetypes containing shapes can be created by making four new linetypes and use shapes from:

a) the AutoCAD es file
b) our own myshape file

The format for complex linetypes containing shapes is:
> ***NAME, description**
> **A,pen moves,[SHAPENAME,shape file name],pen moves**

Note: **1** The SHAPENAME must be the same as the shape in the file.
       2 The shape file name is the **COMPILED** (i.e. .SHX) name.
We will create a new linetype file for the complex linetypes so:

1 Open your STDA3 standard sheet and refer to Fig. 7.9

2 At the command line enter **SHELL** <R> and:
prompt	OS Command
enter	**EDIT :\R13CUST\MYLINSHP.LIN** <R>
prompt	MS DOS text editor
respond	enter the following lines with <R>

          *PNPLINE,---[PNP]---[PNP]
          A,1,-0.25,[PNP,es.shx],-1
          *ANDLINE,using the AND symbol
          A,2,-2,[AND,es.shx],-1
          *POGOLINE,---[POGO]---[POGO]
          A,2,-0.5,[POGO,myshape.shx],-2.5
          *CROSS,using the CROSS symbol
          A,2,-0.5,[CROSS,myshape.shx],-2.5

3 File–Save As the File–Exit to return to drawing.

4 The complete linetype file is also listed in fig. (a).

5 New linetypes must be loaded before they can be used so:
    a) make four new layers, e.g. L1, L2, etc.
    b) set a new linetype on each new layer
    c) the new linetype file must be loaded
    d) you may be prompted to load the es.shx shape file?

6 Using each new layer/linetype, create some entities as fig. (b) and fig. (c). The global LTSCALE value was set to 12, and the ltScale option of the CHANGE command was used to optimize the linetype appearance.

7 Save your work if required.

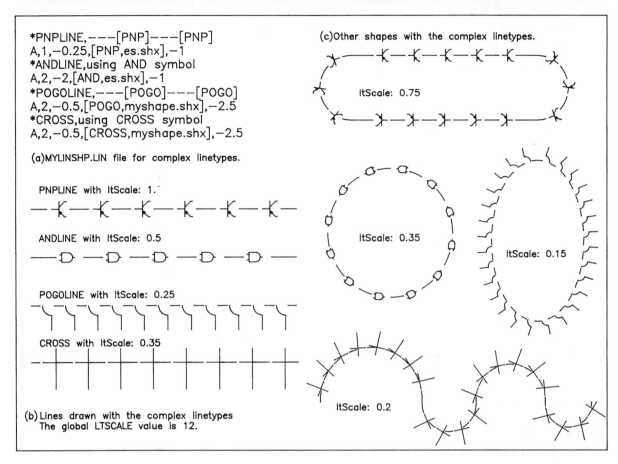

```
*PNPLINE,---[PNP]---[PNP]
A,1,-0.25,[PNP,es.shx],-1
*ANDLINE,using AND symbol
A,2,-2,[AND,es.shx],-1
*POGOLINE,---[POGO]---[POGO]
A,2,-0.5,[POGO,myshape.shx],-2.5
*CROSS,using CROSS symbol
A,2,-0.5,[CROSS,myshape.shx],-2.5
```

(a)MYLINSHP.LIN file for complex linetypes.

PNPLINE with ltScale: 1.

ANDLINE with ltScale: 0.5

POGOLINE with ltScale: 0.25

CROSS with ltScale: 0.35

(b)Lines drawn with the complex linetypes
The global LTSCALE value is 12.

(c)Other shapes with the complex linetypes.

ltScale: 0.75

ltScale: 0.35

ltScale: 0.15

ltScale: 0.2

Figure 7.9 Complex linetypes containing shapes.

Summary

1 Shape creation and usage involves:
  a) drawing the shapes with drawing unit sizes
  b) coding the shapes
  c) creating the .SHP shape file
  d) compiling the .SHX file
  e) loading the compiled file
  f) using the SHAPE command.
2 The shape definition is:
  *Number,Bytes,NAME
  coded definitions
3 The shape commands can be activated:
  a) *Compiling:* Menu bar with Tools–Compile...
    Command line with COMPILE
  b) *Loading:* Menu bar with Data–Shape File...
    Command line with LOAD
  c) *Using:* Shape icon from the Miscellaneous toolbar
    Command line with SHAPE
4 Special codes exist for specific usage:
  001:    pen down, i.e. draw
  002:    pen up, i.e. do not draw
  008:    single X,Y displacement
  009:    multiple X,Y displacements
  010:    octant arcs.
5 All shape definitions end with a 0.
6 The 009 code ends with (0,0).
7 The number of bytes in the first line of the shape definition is the total number of bytes in the second line.
8 Shape numbers in any file must be between 1 and 255.
9 The codes 001,002,008,009,00A are usually shortened to 1,2,8,9,10.
10 The pen is always assumed to be down.
11 I generally always create shapes with the pen down and 'draw over' existing lines.
12 When an existing shape file has been altered, it is necessary to exit AutoCAD then re-open the drawing.

Activity

For the shape activity we will return to the computer shop. One of the computers in the shop window was displaying a game and we will add some pixels as shapes.

Refer to Tutorial 7 and:

1 Draw the computer to your own size.

2 Create the five new shapes in a file COMP.SHP. The shape names and sizes (as drawing units) are given.

3 Compile the COMP.SHP file.

4 Load the compiled shape file.

5 Use the shape command to add the five shapes to the computer monitor, using your imagination for the layout.

Chapter 8

Slides

When a drawing is opened a file with the extension .DWG is displayed. This file may contain information about dimensions, layers, attributes, etc. and all this data must be processed before the drawing can be viewed on the screen. This takes time and uses memory.

AutoCAD contains a facility to 'capture' drawings as photographic snapshots called *SLIDES* with several advantages to the user:

1 they are easy to make
2 quickly viewed
3 do not use much memory
4 allow several pictures of the one drawing to be stored for future recall.

Slides are files with the extension **.SLD**. They can be created on floppy disk or in a named directory.

Uses for slides

Slides are 'pictures' of the drawing screen and once created, **cannot be modified**. They can be used for many purposes, some of which are:
1 Running a slide show.
2 Making a slide library.
3 Creating hatch icons.
4 For icon menus.
5 Simple animation.
6 Presentation work.
7 Project work.

In this chapter we will investigate several of these options with worked examples.

Note

1 While slides are very easy to make, the process is very repetitive and can become rather tedious.
2 Slides are generally used with script files (next chapter), so their full potential will not be evident in this chapter.
3 When creating slides always take a note of the slide names. It is very easy to forget what slides have been created.

Slide example 1: a slide show

A slide show is a series of slides 'run together' with a 'program'. This program is a script file (next chapter) written by the user using a text editor. To run a slide show the slides must obviously have been prepared and we will now create these slides.

Imagine two views of a bearing drawing being 'constructed' and:

1 Start AutoCAD R13 and begin a new drawing with:
   a) Prototype name: C:\R13CUST\STDA3
   b) New Drawing Name: C:\R13CUST\FLANGE

2 This will open your STDA3 standard sheet.

3 Refer to Fig. 8.1.

Creating the slides

1 With layer CL current draw two centre lines:
   a) horizontal: from 20,140; to @340,0
   b) vertical: from 120,240; to @0,−200
   c) fig. (a).

2 From the menu bar select **Tools–Slide–Save...** and:
   prompt Create Slide File dialogue box
   respond *a*) check directory c:\r13cust
           b) enter File name as **FL1** (or fl1)
           c) pick OK.

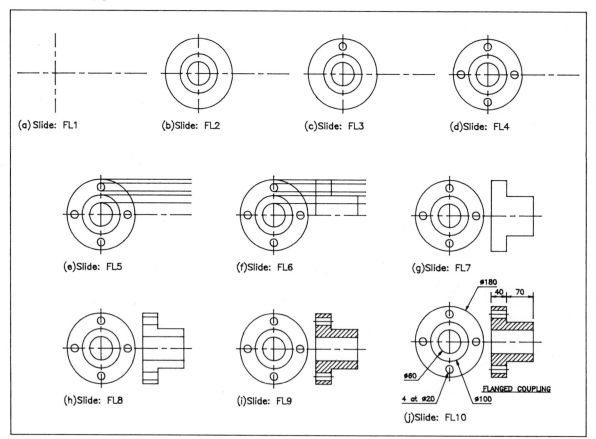

(a) Slide: FL1   (b) Slide: FL2   (c) Slide: FL3   (d) Slide: FL4

(e) Slide: FL5   (f) Slide: FL6   (g) Slide: FL7

(h) Slide: FL8   (i) Slide: FL9   (j) Slide: FL10

Figure 8.1 Stages in constructing slides FL1–FL10 for slide show.

3 With layer OUT current, draw three concentric circles at the centre line intersection with radii of 90, 50 and 30 – fig. (b).

4 At the command line enter **MSLIDE** <R> and:

prompt   Create Slide File dialogue box

with   fl1.sld listed

respond *a*) directory c;\r13cust?

         b) enter File name as **fl2**

         c) pick OK

Note: *a*) slides are created using:

           i) Tools–Slide–Save...

           ii) MSLIDE at the command line

         b) both options display the Create Slide File dialogue box

         c) it is user preference as to what method is used.

5 Add a bolt hole, centre at 120,210 and radius 10 – fig. (c). Make a slide FL3.

6 Polar array the red bolt hole:

  a) about the large circle centre

  b) for four items

  c) full 360 angle

  d) with rotation – fig. (d).

7 Make a slide (FL4) of the arrayed holes.

8 Make layer CONS current and draw five horizontal lines (length 240) as fig. (e).

9 Make a new slide named FL5.

10 With layer OUT current again, draw the top half of the right-hand view (five lines), the 'widths' being 40 and 70 – fig. (f). Make a slide of the complete view as FL6.

11 *a*) Delete the five construction lines.

  b) Mirror the five red outlines about the green horizontal centre line, without deleting old objects – fig. (g).

  c) Make a slide FL7.

12 Add to the right view:

  a) four horizontal bolt hole lines on layer OUT

  b) two horizontal lines for the shaft on layer OUT

13 Make a slide of fig. (h) named FL8.

14 *a*) with layer CL current draw two bolt hole centre lines

  b) with SECT layer current, add hatching to the four areas using User Defined, 45 angle and 4 spacing – fig. (i)

  c) Make a slide of the component named FL9.

15 Finally, add some dimensions (on layer DIM) and a title (on layer TEXT) as fig. (j). Make your last slide FL10.

16 This completes the slide creation stage.

17 At this stage select **File-Save** from the menu bar to save the complete drawing as C:\R13CUST\FLANGE.

Viewing the slides

Now that the slides have been created, they can be viewed so:

1 Still with drawing FLANGE on the screen?

2 From the menu bar select **Tools–Slide–View...** and:
   prompt   Select Slide File dialogue box
   respond   *a*) check directory c:\r13cust
          b) pick **fl5.sld** file
          c) pick OK.

3 The screen displays the left view with the five construction lines.

4 At the command line enter **VSLIDE** <R> and:
   prompt   Select Slide File dialogue box
   respond   pick slide **fl8.sld** then OK

5 Screen displays two views prior to hatching.

6 Pick the REDRAW icon and the original component will be displayed.

7 At present this is all we can achieve with slides.

Note

1 Slides are 'pictures' of the screen and CANNOT be modified. View any one of your slides and try and erase any entity – you cannot.

2 There are only three commands used with slides:
   a) Make with MSLIDE or Tools–Slide–Save
   b) View with VSLIDE of Tools–Slide–View
   c) Redraw to restore the original screen.

Slide example 2: an animation

An animation is similar to a slide show as it requires both slides and a script file. The example I have selected is a simple representation of a reciprocating engine and we will prepare the slides in preparation for the next chapter (script files).

1 Start AutoCAD and from the menu bar select **File–New** and at the New Drawing Name box enter:
   C:\R13CUST\RECIP=C:\R13CUST\STDA3 <R>

2 This will open your STDA3 standard sheet.

3 Refer to Fig. 8.2 which displays eight stages in one revolution of the crankshaft – every 45 degrees.

4 With layer OUT current, draw the arrangement to the sizes in fig. (a) positioning the component in the centre of the screen – do not add dimensions.

5 From the menu bar select **File–Save** which will save the screen drawing as C:\R13CUST\RECIP (step 1)

6 Make a slide of this position and:
   a) ensure directory is c:\r13cust
   b) slide name is RECIP1.

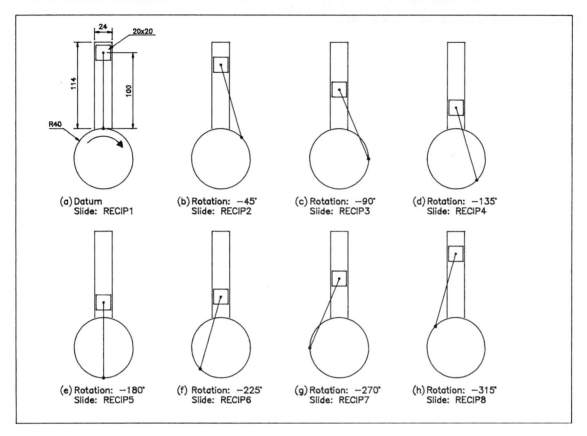

Figure 8.2 Stages in construction of slides for animation.

7 Reposition the piston/connecting rod as fig. (b) for a rotation of 45 degrees and make a slide named RECIP2. Obtaining this position requires some thought. My method was to:
a) rotate the crank donut on the circle by −45 degrees
b) draw a circle of radius 100, centred on the donut
c) draw a vertical line through the piston 'centre'
d) draw a line from new donut position to intersection of the 100 circle and the vertical line
e) erase unwanted entities.

8 Make a slide of this new position, the name being RECIP2.

9 Repeat the repositioning of the piston/con rod making a slide of each new position, the names being:

rotation	(total)	slide	fig.
−45	−90	RECIP3	(c)
−45	−135	RECIP4	(d)
−45	−180	RECIP5	(e)
−45	−225	RECIP6	(f)
−45	−270	RECIP7	(g)
−45	−315	RECIP8	(h)

10 At present the slides can be viewed, but we cannot prepare the animation until the next chapter.

11 *Note. a*)   If you are feeling really adventurous, you could make a slide for every 15 degree rotation. This will greatly improve your animation.
  b)   I told you that creating slides could be boring!

Slide example 3: a slide library

A slide presentation may contain dozens of slides and this can result in disks and directories becoming congested with .SLD files. In our two slide examples we have already created 18 slide files, and will create more before this chapter is finished. When working with slides it is useful to keep all related slides in a slide library. To create a slide library it is necessary to use a utility program called **SLIDELIB**. We have created two sets of slides (flange and reciprocating) and will use these to create two slide libraries.

During this exercise I had to enter the DOS environment as I could not complete certain parts of it while running AutoCAD. The sequence of operations is:

1 Exit Windows and enter DOS, i.e. C:\> prompt.

2 Change the directory with:
CD\R13\COM\SUPPORT <R> where R13 is the Release 13 directory.

3 At the command line enter **DIR *.EXE** <R> and:
prompt   DXFIX   EXE
          SLIDELIB EXE

Note: if SLIDELIB.EXE is not listed on your system you will not be able to complete this exercise. Proceed to slide example 4.

4 Copy the slide library program into your directory with:
COPY SLIDELIB.EXE C:\R13CUST <R>

5 Change to your directory with:
CD\R13CUST <R>

6 At the command line enter **EDIT** <R> and:
prompt   MS DOS text editor
enter   **FL1.SLD** <R>
          FL2.SLD <R>
          FL3.SLD <R>, etc. until **FL10.SLD**
then   File–Save As and:
          a) check directory C:\R13CUST
          b) enter File Name as **FLANGE.TXT**
          c) pick OK
          d) File–Exit to return to DOS (C:\R13CUST).

7 Create another new file with EDIT and:
enter   **RECIP1.SLD** <R>
          RECIP2.SLD <R>
          RECIP3.SLD, etc. until **RECIP8.SLD**
then   File–Save As and:
          a) directory C:\R13CUST
          b) enter File Name as **RECIP.TXT**
          c) pick OK
          d) File-Exit to return to DOS.

8 At the C:\R13CUST prompt enter:
SLIDELIB FLANGLIB<FLANGE.TXT <R>

prompt   SLIDELIB 1.2 (3/8/89)
         (C) Copyright AutoDESK

9 Repeat the slide library command with:
SLIDELIB RECIPLIB<RECIP.TXT <R>

10 At the prompt line enter **DIR *.SLB** <R> and:
FLANGLIB SLB 9866(?)   date time
RECIPLIB SLB 5899(?)   date time

11 *Explanation.*
The line SLIDELIB FLANGLIB<FLANGE.TXT may require some discussion for several readers who are not familiar with DOS.
a) SLIDELIB: the utility program being 'run'
b) FLANGLIB: the name of the library file being created
c) FLANGE.TXT: the source text file containing the slides
d) <: a directional indicator meaning 'transfer all data from the file FLANGE.TXT into the file named FLANGLIB'
e) the extension **.SLB** is automatically added during the operation and is a compiled extension name, i.e. FLANGLIB.SLB is a compiled version of FLANGE.TXT.

12 *Using the slide library.*
a) Change back to the C: drive, enter Windows.
b) Start AutoCAD R13 and open your STDA3 standard sheet.
c) From the menu bar select **Tools-Slide-View...** and:

prompt	Select Slide File dialogue box
respond	pick **Type it**
prompt	Slide file
enter	**FLANGLIB(FL8)** <R>
prompt	Slide of flanged coupling - two views with hatching
respond	pick **Redraw** icon

d) at the command line enter **VSLIDE** <R> and:

prompt	Select Slide File dialogue box
respond	pick **Type it**
prompt	Slide name
enter	**RECIPLIB(RECIP5)** <R>
prompt	Slide of engine at bottom of stroke
respond	pick **Redraw** icon to return to drawing screen.

13 *Notes*:
a) the slides FL1.SLD; RECIP1.SLD, etc. are still available for viewing.
b) the slide library procedure may seem rather involved but:
   i) it is good 'housekeeping'
   ii) all relevant slides are kept together in their own named library
   iii) the process stops disk/directories becoming full of .SLD files.

14 This completes the slide library exercise.

Slide example 4: slides for an icon menu

Slides can be created for use in an icon menu. We will investigate menus in a later chapter but will prepare the slides in this exercise, so:

1 Open your STDA3 standard sheet and refer to Fig. 8.3 which displays four icons to be used in a housing estate layout.

2 With layer OUT current, use the given sizes and draw the four icons using discretion for any omitted dimensions. Position your icons anywhere on the screen.

3 Make blocks of the four icons:
a) using the NAME given, e.g. SEMI
b) with the block insertion point at the top left corner of each icon.

4 At this stage save your drawing as **C:\R13CUST\ESTATE** for future recall.

5 Insert the block SEMI:
a) at the insertion point 20,50
b) full size, i.e. X=Y=1
c) with 0 rotation.

6 Zoom-Window from 0,0 to 90,60.

7 Make a slide of the screen (the zoomed area) with the name SEMI.

8 Erase the SEMI block.

9 Insert the block 3BED at the point 20,50 full size with 0 rotation.

10 Make a slide of the screen using the name 3BED.

11 Erase the block.

12 Repeat steps 9–11 for the blocks 4BED and FLAT using the names 4BED and FLAT for the slide names.

13 At present we cannot continue with this exercise so proceed to the last slide example.

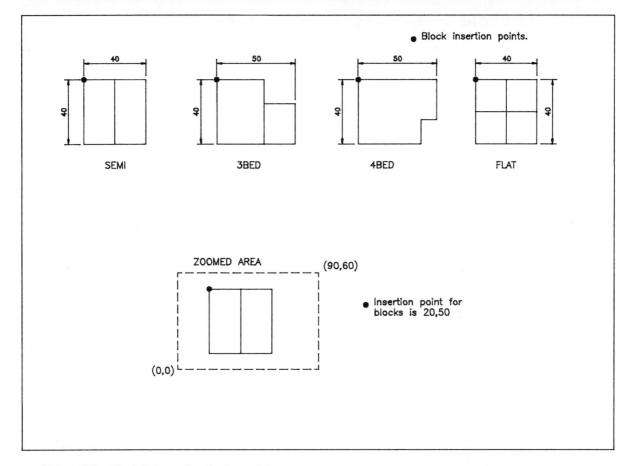

Figure 8.3 Block information for icon slides.

Slide example 5: slides for hatch patterns

This example is very similar to exercise 4. We will create a series of slides which will allow our created hatch patterns to be used in icon form. The icon slides cannot be used until we have discussed menus, but at least the slides will have been created.

1 Open your standard sheet (STDA3) and refer to Fig. 8.4.

2 Erase the border and draw a rectangle from 0,0 with length 90 and width 60.

3 Zoom in on the area 0,0 to 90,60.

4 At the command line enter **HATCH** <R> and:
   prompt   Pattern... and enter **TSHAPE** <R>
   prompt   Scale... and enter **2** <R>
   prompt   Angle... and enter **0** <R>
   prompt   Select objects and pick the four lines of the rectangle
   then   <R>

5 The TSHAPE hatching will be added to the zoomed rectangle.

6 Make a slide of the screen, the name being TSHAPE.

7 Erase the added hatching.

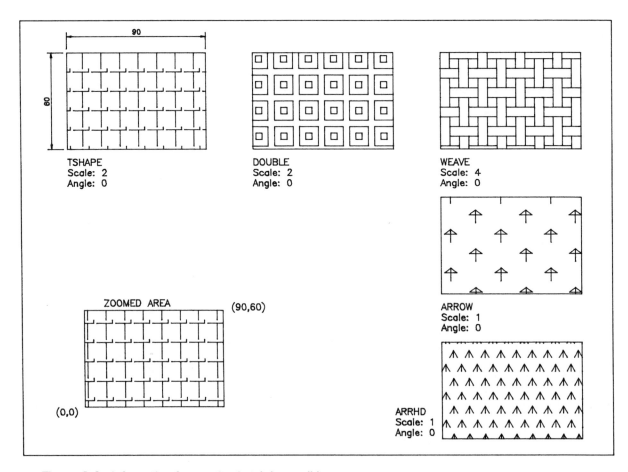

Figure 8.4 Information for creating hatch icons slides.

8 Repeat steps 4–7 for your other created hatch patterns using the following data:

Pattern	Scale	Angle	Slide name
DOUBLE	2	0	DOUBLE
WEAVE	4	0	WEAVE
ARROW	1	0	ARROW
ARRHD	1	0	ARRHD

Note: ARRHD is the hatch pattern activity. If you did not create this pattern then do not enter any data for it.

9 This completes the last slide example.

Summary

1 Slides are 'snapshots' of the drawing screen.
2 Slides cannot be modified.
3 Slides are created and viewed with:
   a) menu bar Tools–Slide–Save/View
   b) command line MSLIDE/VSLIDE
4 Related slides can be stored in a slide library.
5 Redraw will restore the drawing screen.
6 Slides have many uses.
7 The full benefit of slides will not be apparent until we have discussed script files and menus.

Activity

The activity for this chapter requires you to make two new slide libraries for the hatch and house slides, so:

1 Using slide Example 3 (steps 5–7) make the following new text files in your C:\R13CUST directory:
   a) HOUSE.TXT: containing the four house slides
   b) HATCH.TXT: containing the four (or five) hatch slides.

2 Using the SLIDELIB command (steps 8–9) create two new slide libraries for:
   a) HOUSELIB: from HOUSE.TXT
   b) HATCHLIB: from HATCH.TXT.

3 These slide libraries will be used in another chapter.

Chapter 9

Script files

Script files are text files written by the user to:
1 run slide shows and animations
2 display drawing routines
3 execute frequently used routines.

Script file commands

Script files are written using a text editor and have the extension **.SCR**. There are only a few commands used with them, the most common being:

VSLIDE xxx   displays the slide named xxx
DELAY nnn   gives a pause between lines in a script file. The delay is *nnn milliseconds*, the user specifying the value of nnn
RSCRIPT   returns to the first line of the script file, i.e. reruns the complete file ESC stops a script file SCRIPT the command to select a script file.

Script example 1: a slide show

1 Open your FLANGE drawing saved during the previous chapter.

2 At the command line enter **SHELL** <R> and:
     prompt   OS Command
     enter   **EDIT C:\R13CUST\FLANGE.SCR** <R>
     prompt   MS DOS text screen
     enter   the following, remembering to <RETURN> *immediately* after the line entry:
         VSLIDE FL1 <R>
         DELAY 2000
         VSLIDE FL2
         DELAY 2000
         VSLIDE FL3
         DELAY 2000
         VSLIDE FL4
         DELAY 2000
         VSLIDE FL5
         DELAY 2000
         VSLIDE FL6
         DELAY 2000
         VSLIDE FL7
         DELAY 2000
         VSLIDE FL8
         DELAY 2000
         VSLIDE FL9
         DELAY 2000
         VSLIDE FL10
         DELAY 5000
         RSCRIPT

then   *a*) File–Save As, check directory and name then pick OK.

           b) File–Exit to return to drawing.

           c) From the menu bar select **Tools–Run Script...**

prompt   Select `Script File` dialogue box

respond   *a*) check directory c:\r13cust

           b) pick file **flange.scr**

           c) pick OK.

4 The 10 slides of the flanged component will be displayed with a short pause between each one, allowing you to 'talk through' the slides as the component is being constructed.

5 When you are 'bored' with the slide show press **ESC** to stop it.

6 Pick the REDRAW icon to restore the original FLANGE drawing.

7 *Notes*.

    a) The delay number can be increased/decreased as required.

    b) DELAY 1000 gives about a 1 second pause.

    c) The slides could have text items added to assist with the component construction?

8 *Task*.

Before leaving this exercise:

a) Select from the menu bar File-New and:

     i)   pick No to save changes

     ii)   pick OK at the Create New Drawing dialogue box.

b) From menu bar select Tools-Run Script... and:

     prompt   Select `Slide File` dialogue box

     respond   *i*)   change directory to **c:\r13cust**

                ii)   pick file **flange.scr**

                iii)   pick OK

     prompt   Text Window with `Can't open file` message and a list of directories?

c) To run a slide show it is necessary to open a drawing from the directory containing the slides and the script file.

9 Now proceed to the next exercise.

Script example 2: an animation

This example is really the same as the first example, but the script has no delays.

1 Open your saved RECIP drawing of the piston arrangement.

2 At the command line enter **SHELL** <R> and:

    prompt   `OS Command`

    enter   **EDIT C:\R13CUST\RECIP.SCR** <R>

    prompt   `MS DOS` text screen

    enter   the following lines, remembering <RETURN>

            VSLIDE RECIP1 <R>

            VSLIDE RECIP2

            VSLIDE RECIP3

            VSLIDE RECIP4

            VSLIDE RECIP5

            VSLIDE RECIP6

            VSLIDE RECIP7

            VSLIDE RECIP8

            RSCRIPT

    then   File–Save As to save the file (pick OK) File–Exit to return to drawing.

3 At the command line enter **SCRIPT** <R> and:
  prompt   Select Script File dialogue box
  respond   *a*) check directory is c:\r13cust
       b) pick file **recip.scr**
       c) pick OK.

4 The piston arrangement slides will be displayed one after the other and as there are no delays between the slides you have an apparent animation.

5 Press ESC to stop the animation and Redraw icon to restore the original drawing.

6 *Notes*.
  a) the 'jerky' effect could be reduced by having more slides in the script file, i.e. slides every 10/15 degree of rotation
  b) the 'flicker' effect cannot really be removed. Perhaps removing the original drawing border would help?

Script example 3: a drawing routine

Script files can be written which will produce a drawing, so:

1 Open your STDA3 standard sheet.

2 At the command line enter **SHELL** <R> and:
  prompt   OS Command
  enter   **EDIT C:\R13CUST\DRAW.SCR** <R>
  prompt   Text editor
  respond   enter the following lines, ensuring that there are no spaces between the last line entry and the <R> press:
       ;a drawing sequence
       COLOUR RED<R>
       PLINE 10,10 W 10 10 370,10 370,260 10,260 C<R>
       COLOUR BLUE<R>
       DONUT 50 60 90,200 290,200 190,115 <R>
       <R>
       COLOUR GREEN<R>
       PLINE 90,200 W 5 5 290,200 190,50 C<R>
       COLOUR MAGENTA<R>
       DONUT 20 40 115,50 265,50 <R>
       <R>
       COLOUR 9<R>
       PLINE 115,50 W 2 2 265,50 190,195<R>
       DELAY 20000<R>
       ERASE C 10,10 370,260<R>
       <R>
       REDRAW<R>

3 *a*) File–Save As checking directory and file name.
  b) File–Exit to return to drawing.

4 Activate the SCRIPT command (menu bar or direct entry) and select/pick the file **draw.scr**.

5 The drawing example will be displayed on the screen for a few seconds then it will be erased.

6 *Notes.*

   a) This script file uses the AutoCAD commands as they would be used from the keyboard.

   b) Coordinates are specified as 10,10, etc.

   c) Spaces in lines are equivalent to <R> in a command sequence.

   d) A blank line (<R>) signifies the use of the <RETURN> key at the end of the previous line – think about this!

   e) The two lines at DONUT 20 40 115,50 265,50 <R> are thus:

DONUT	the AutoCAD command name
space	<R> after the command DONUT
20	the inner diameter
space	<R> after entering 20
40	the outer diameter
space	<R> after entering 40
115,50	coordinates of donut centre
space	<R> after entering 115,50
265,50	coordinates of another donut
space	<R> after entering 265,50
<R>	end of text line
<R>	next line <RETURN> is equivalent to cancelling the donut command.

   f) To write lines in this type of file, the user records every entry for each command to be used, i.e. you try the sequence manually from the keyboard, noting every step as it happens.

   g) Comments can be added using the semicolon (;) at the start of a line, e.g. the first line in the file.

Script example 4: a user routine

Frequently used routines can be made into script files and run at any time. To demonstrate this, we will write a file to set an A4 standard sheet with layers, so:

1 Begin a New drawing, accepting the prototype name.

2 Ensure all linetypes are loaded.

3 At the command line enter **SHELL** <R> and:

prompt	OS Command
enter	**EDIT C:\R13CUST\A4SETUP.SCR** <R>
prompt	MS DOS screen
respond	enter the following lines:

   ;A4 SET UP<R>
   BLIPMODE OFF<R>
   UNITS 2 2 1 0 0 N<R>
   GRID 10<R>
   SNAP 5<R>
   LTSCALE 10<R>
   LAYER M OUT N CL,HID,DIM,TEXT<R>
   <R>
   LAYER C 1 OUT C 3 CL C 4 HID C 5 DIM C 6 TEXT<R>
   <R>
   LAYER L CENTER CL L HIDDEN HID<R>
   <R>
   LIMITS 0,0 297,200<R>
   LINE 0,0 285,0 285,190 0,190 C<R>
   ZOOM A<R>

then   *a*) `File-Save As.......`
           b) `File-Exit.`

4 Activate the SCRIPT command and pick the file **a4setup.scr**.

5 The script file will set units to decimal, set grid and snap on, blips off, make new layers with colours and linetypes,set the A4 limits, then draw a border.

6 Check the Layer Control dialogue box.

7 This completes the exercise for script files.

Summary

1 Script files are text files written by the user.
2 Script files are used for:
    a) slide shows and animation's
    b) programmed drawing routines
    c) frequently used 'operations'.
3 Script files are activated:
    a) from the menu bar with Tools-Run Script...
    b) with SCRIPT at the command line.

Activity

No activity for script files.

Chapter 10

Customizing menus

AutoCAD Release 13 has a very comprehensive user-friendly menu structure, and the standard menu layout should be sufficient for all users most of the time. An occasion may arise when it is necessary to change the menu structure to suit your own 'advanced' skills or to meet a customer's requirements. There are different 'types' of menus within AutoCAD and users will be familiar with most of them without (perhaps) knowing their names. The menu types are:

a) screen menus
b) pull-down menus (menu bar items)
c) pop-up menu dialogue boxes
d) cascade menus
e) icon (image tile) menus
f) tablet menus
g) toolbars
h) keyboard accelerators
i) pointing device button menus.

Menu customization can be achieved in two ways:
1 by adding to the existing AutoCAD menu
2 by creating a new menu.

In this chapter we will investigate several of the menu types by creating our own customized menu, building it up in stages as more options are considered. This will allow the existing menu system to remain untouched – a wise precaution?

AutoCAD R13's menus

To investigate the existing menu structure within AutoCAD:

1 Start up and open your standard sheet.

2 At the command line enter **FILES** <R> and:
prompt   File Utilities dialogue box
respond   pick **List Files...**
prompt   File List dialogue box
respond   *a*) pick the **r13** directory
          b) pick **win** sub-directory
          c) pick **support** sub-directory (i.e. **r13\win\support** is directory name – note this).

4 Change File name to ***.mn?** then <R>
prompt   list of AutoCAD menus:
          acad.mnc acadfull.mnc
          acad.mnr acadfull.mnl
          acad.mns acadfull.mnr
          acad.mnu acadfull.mns
                   acadfull.mnu
respond   study the menu list then:
          a) Cancel the File List dialogue box.
          b) Exit the File Utilities dialogue box.

3 *Notes.*

a) AutoCAD has two menu structures:

i)   acad: the short menu

ii)   acadfull: the full menu with more options.

b) the menu file extensions are:

.mnu: template menu file written by the user

.mnc: compiled menu file used by AutoCAD. It contains the commands and appearance of the menu to be used

.mnr: resource menu file containing the bitmaps to be used by the created menu

.mns: source menu file modified by AutoCAD as the changes to the menu are made.

c) there are two other menu file extensions:

i)   .mnl: menu LISP files containing AutoLISP expressions

ii)   .mnd: menu definition files and are special menu source files containing macros.

d) the only menu file that the user is concerned with is the **.mnu** template file. AutoCAD compiles the .mnc and .mnr files itself and modifies the .mns file as a drawing is being created.

First menu: a screen menu

Most users will probably be using the Windows Release 13 without a screen menu, but the facility exists within R13 to display screen menus. Our first menu example will be to create a simple screen menu and we will write it, use it and then discuss it.

1   Open your STDA3 standard sheet and cancel all toolbars.

2   From the menu bar select **Options**

                           Preferences...

prompt   Preferences dialogue box

with   System card active

respond   **Activate the Screen menu** (i.e. X in box)

then   OK.

3   The drawing screen will be returned with a screen menu at the right displaying File–Help, the same as the menu bar?

4   At the command line enter **SHELL** <R> and:

prompt   OS Command

enter   **EDIT :\R13CUST\MYMENU.MNU** <R>

prompt   MS DOS text editor

respond   enter the following lines as given (the line numbers are for reference and should not be included in the menu)

***SCREEN<R>	line 1
[MYMENU]<R>	line 2
<R>	line 3
[LINE] ^C^C_LINE<R>	line 4
[CIRCLE] ^C^C_CIRCLE<R>	line 5
[ERASE] ^C^C_ERASE<R>	line 6

5   File–Save As checking the directory and file name.

6   File–Exit to return to the drawing screen.

7 At the command line enter **MENU** <R> and:
prompt Select Menu File dialogue box
respond *a*) change directory to **r13cust**
    b) scroll down at List Files of Type
    c) pick Menu Template (*.MNU)
    d) pick **mymenu.mnu**
    e) pick OK
        prompt   AutoCAD message as Fig. 10.1 – don't panic
        respond   read it and then pick OK.

8 The drawing screen will display your standard sheet with your menu at the right side with the commands LINE, CIRCLE and ERASE.

9 Note the menu bar only displays File and Help.

10 Use your screen commands to draw some line and circle entities, erasing as required – Fig. 10.2(a).

11 At this stage save your drawing as **MYDRAWG** and exit AutoCAD.

12 *Notes*.
    a) At present the right-hand button on the mouse will not work as it has not yet been 'programmed'. This means that you need to use the <RETURN> key to cancel commands. This is a nuisance but will be rectified in the next menu.
    b) All AutoCAD commands can still be used with direct entry from the keyboard, e.g. Enter PLINE <R> and prompt: From point....., etc.
    c) The line and circle entities being drawn should be red if you have opened STDA3. Why is this?

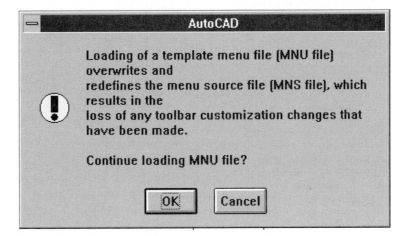

Figure 10.1 AutoCAD menu file message.

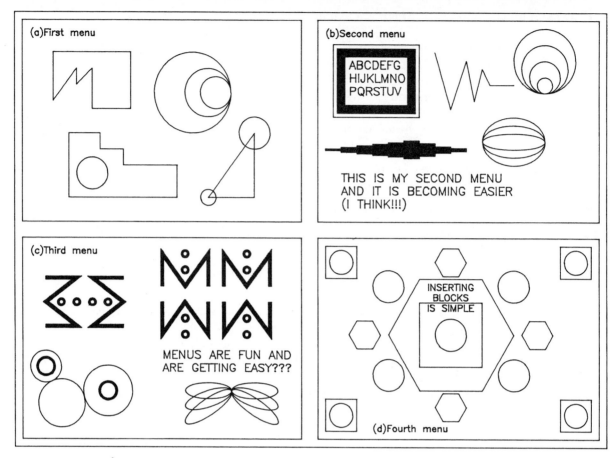

Figure 10.2 Using the customized menu MYMEM.MNU.

Menu explanation

Line	Item	Discussion
1	***SCREEN	Signifies a screen menu. The *** are section labels and will be used in other menus
2	[MYMENU]	The menu title placed in [] brackets.
3	\<R\>	Gives a blank line on the screen.
4	[LINE]^C^C_LINE	[LINE]: display LINE on screen

5 [CIRCLE]^C^C_CIRCLE   this line can be read as: Display the word CIRCLE on the screen and when selected:

Line 4 discussion continued:
^C^C: cancel any active command
_: a spacer only and does nothing.
LINE: the AutoCAD command.

Line 5 discussion continued:
a) cancel any active command with ^C^C
b) activate the AutoCAD CIRCLE command.

6 [ERASE]^C^C_ERASE   Display the word ERASE on the screen and when selected:
a) cancel any active command with ^C^C
b) activate the AutoCAD ERASE command.

Note

All menus are basically written as above. Items placed within **[ ]** brackets are displayed in the screen menu area (or pull-down area as you will soon discover). A maximum of eight characters is allowed within the [ ] brackets. The ^C^C (^C is shift 6) is used to cancel any active command and has been inherited from pre-R13 versions when ^C was the cancel command before the ESC key. Some commands need a double cancel (e.g. DIM) and hence *^C^C is used after every [ ] item*. Using the AutoCAD commands (e.g. LINE, CIRCLE, etc.) is sensible as they are all in memory and we will use them in all written menus. Hopefully the menu idea will become easier to you as additions are made to this basic menu.

Second menu: the right button, more screen option and a pull-down

This menu will build up on the first menu by adding additional items to the screen selection, adding a pull-down and the 'program' of the right button of the mouse to cancel commands.

1 Start AutoCAD and note the screen layout. It should be as you left it after saving your first menu drawing with your screen menu displayed at the right.

2 From the menu bar select **File–Open** and:
a) directory **c:\r13cust**
b) pick **mydrawg.dwg** file
c) pick OK.

3 Your drawing using the first menu should be displayed.

4 At the command line enter **SHELL** <R> then: **EDIT C:\R13CUST\MYMENU.MNU** <R> to display your first menu in the MS DOS text editor.

5 Add the following additional lines to the file, noting that I have listed the complete file and added an (N) for the new lines.
Remember <RETURN> **IMMEDIATELY** after the line entry.

***AUX1	N
;	N
***SCREEN	
[MYMENU]	
<R>	
[LINE]^C^C_LINE	
[CIRCLE]^C^C_CIRCLE	
[ERASE]^C^C_ERASE	
<R>	N
[ZOOMWIND]^C^C_ZOOM W	N
[ZOOM ALL]^C^C_ZOOM A	N
***POP1	N
[DRAWING]	N
[LINE]^C^C_LINE	N
[DTEXT]^C^C_DTEXT	N
[PLINE]^C^C_PLINE	N
[ELLIPSE]^C^C_ELLIPSE	N

6 File–Save As then File–Exit, etc.

7 At the command line enter **MENU** <R> and:

> *prompt*   Select `Menu File` dialogue box noting two files:
>> *a*) mymenu.mnc – compiled
>> *b*) mymenu.mns – source.
>
> *respond*   *a*) pick Menu Template (*.MNU)
>> *b*) pick **mymenu.mnu**
>> *c*) pick OK
>
> *prompt*   AutoCAD menu message again
> *respond*   pick OK.

8 The drawing screen will be displayed with:

a) the two additional ZOOM items in the screen menu area
b) DRAWING in the menu bar.

9 *Questions*:

> a) why did we re-select mymenu.mnu?
> b) why no File–Help in menu bar?
> c) how do we save/open a drawing?

10 Using your screen and menu bar items, erase the existing entities then draw new entities by referring to Fig. 10.2(b). Try the ZOOMWIND and ZOOM ALL screen menu selections. Does the right-button on the mouse work?

11 At the command line enter **SAVE** <R> and:

> *prompt*   `Save Drawing As` dialogue box
> *respond*   pick OK to update MYDRAWG answering **Yes** to the replace existing file message.

12 At the command line enter **MENU** <R> and:

> *prompt*   `Select Menu File` dialogue box
> *respond*   *a*) pick **r13** directory
>> *b*) pick **win** sub-directory
>> *c*) pick **support** sub-directory
>> *d*) pick **acadfull.mnc** file
>> *e*) pick OK.

13 The drawing screen is displayed with:

a) full menu bar selection
b) toolbars (perhaps?)
c) the AutoCAD screen menu
d) your drawing.

14 Now exit AutoCAD.

Second menu notes

1 The first two lines of the second menu are new. ***AUX1 is an auxiliary menu item used for the mouse. The left button on the mouse is always automatically active, and the semi-colon (;) in the second line activates the right button. If you have a three-button mouse, then you would write:

***AUX1
;   – second button active
;   – third button active.

2 Two new items have been added to the screen menu to allow the zoom window and zoom all commands to be selected.

3 The lines from ***POP1 onwards are the pull-down menu, the format being the same as the screen menu:

***POP1:	signifies a pull-down menu in position one. Pull-down menus can be placed in positions 0–16.
[DRAWING]:	the line after ***POP is usually used to display text in the menu bar. Items enclosed in [ ] are displayed.
[LINE]:	display the word LINE in the pull-down area
^C^C_:	cancel any active command.
LINE:	the AutoCAD command.

4 Thus [PLINE]^C^C_PLINE can be read as:
Display the word PLINE and when selected, cancel any active command then activate the AutoCAD PLINE command.

5 The rest of the second menu should be easy to understand?

Third menu: a cascade effect and two further pull-downs

In this menu we will add a cascade effect to the DRAWING pull-down and add an additional two pull-down menus for altering and viewing drawings. We will not alter the screen menu.

1 Start AutoCAD which should display the traditional menu system, as we ended our last session with this menu displayed.

2 Open your MYDRAWG creation from the second menu.

3 At the command line enter MENU and select **mymenu.mnc** from the c:\r13cust directory. The screen will display the five screen commands with DRAWING in the menu bar.

4 Using SHELL-EDIT C:\R13CUST\MYMENU.MNU, add the following lines to the menu, remembering <RETURN> immediately after the line entry.

After [ELLIPSE]... add:
[DONUT]^C^C_DONUT
[->CIRCLE]
[CENRAD]^C^C_CIRCLE
[TTRAD]^C^C_TTR
[<-THREE]^C^C_CIRCLE 3P
*****POP2**
[ALTERING]
[ERASE]^C^C_ERASE
[ERLAST]^C^C_ERASE L;
[COPY]^C^C_COPY
[MIRROR]^C^C_MIRROR
[ROTATE]^C^C_ROTATE
*****POP3**
[SEEING]
[ZOOMWIN]^C^C_ZOOM W
[ZOOMPRV]^C^C_ZOOM P
[ZOOMALL]^C^C_ZOOM A

5 File–Save As, File–Exit, etc. to return to drawing screen.

6 Enter MENU at the command line and:
  a) c:\r13cust directory
  b) pick Menu Template (*.MNU)
  c) pick mymenu.mnu
  d) pick OK
  e) message again, and OK.

7 The menu bar should display the three pull-downs and:

DRAWING	ALTERING	SEEING
LINE	ERASE	ZOOMWIN
DTEXT	ERLAST	ZOOMPRV
PLINE	COPY	ZOOMALL
ELLIPSE	MIRROR	
DONUT	ROTATE	

CIRCLE: CENRAD
        TTRAD
        THREE

8 Use your new menu to create a drawing – Fig. 10.2(c). then save your work as MYDRAWG.

Third menu notes

1 The two new pull-down menus should present no problems to you, ***POP2 and ***POP3 being the area in the menu bar they have been placed. The titles are ALTERING and SEEING, for obvious reasons?

2 The new item in this menu is the cascade effect for the circle selection. This is achieved using the **->** and **<-** keys within the [ ] brackets:

[->CIRCLE]:   CIRCLE is displayed in pull-down area and (->) indicates that a follow-on is required. This is the cascade effect and (>) is displayed after CIRCLE in the pull-down area.

[<-THREE] :   Displays THREE in the pull-down area and (<-) ends the cascade effect.

3 When the CIRCLE option is selected from the pull-down menu, the (->) activates the cascade effect and displays CENRAD, TTRAD and THREE for selection. The last entry in the cascade always has (<-) to end the effect, i.e. there is a start (->) and a stop (<-).

Fourth menu: another pull-down and inserting predefined blocks

In this menu we will create three blocks and insert them by selection from the screen menu. We will also add a pull-down to allow files to be opened, saved, etc.

1 Open your drawing MYDRAWG and restore the acadfull.mnu. This should give you no trouble?

2 Erase all entities from the screen, then (with SNAP ON) create the following:
  a) a 20 sided square
  b) a circle of radius 20
  c) a hexagon, inscribed in a 20 radius circle.

3 Make blocks of the three shapes using the names SQ, CIR, HEX and pick the 'centre' of each shape as the insertion point.

4 Enter **SHELL-EDIT C:\R13CUST\MYMENU.MNU** and add the lines:

   a) *pull-down*

      after [ZOOMALL]... enter:

      ***POP4
      [FILING]
      [SAVING]^C^C_SAVE
      [OPENING]^C^C_OPEN
      [NEWING]^C^C_NEW
      [QUITING]^C^C_QUIT

   b) *screen*

      after [ZOOM ALL]... in ***SCREEN enter:

      <R>, i.e. blank line
      **[SQUARE]^C^C_INSERT SQ **
      **[CIRCLE]^C^C_INSERT CIR **
      **[HEXAGON]^C^C_INSERT HEX **

5 File–Save As, File–Exit, etc.

6 Using MENU, pick mymenu.mnu then OK.

7 The screen menu will display the three shape names, and the menu bar will have a fourth pull-down area – FILING.

8 Use your new menu with the new shapes – Fig. 10.2(d), then save your drawing using the menu bar FILING–SAVING.

9 Exit AutoCAD from the menu bar FILING–QUITING.

Fourth menu notes

a) The new pull-down (FILING) should be fairly easy to understand as I have used the AutoCAD commands for save, open, new and exit.

b) The screen menu has been used to insert previously created blocks and:

    [SQUARE]:   appears in screen menu area

    ^C^C_: cancels any active command

    INSERT: the AutoCAD command

    SQ: the block name

    \\:   a pause for user input.

Fifth menu: sub-menus, icon menus and dialogue boxes

This menu will allow us to insert previously created blocks from an icon menu as well as investigates how sub-menus are used. We will also create another pull-down to activate dialogue boxes. This menu is quite 'complex' and will involve you in quite a bit of work. The end result is well worth the time and effort spent, and you will be pleasantly surprised with the result.

1 Start AutoCAD and the screen should display your fourth menu. If your menu is not displayed then enter MENU and:
a) check directory is c:\r13cust
b) pick mymenu.mnc
c) pick OK.

2 From the menu bar select FILING-OPENING and pick your **ESTATE** drawing from Chapter 8. This drawing was used to create four house blocks and icon slides.

3 Erase any entities from the screen and refer to Fig. 10.3 which displays an estate layout and four 'tree shapes'.

4 Draw the four tree shapes the maximum diameter being about 30. Use your imagination/expertise with the design (I used a polar array effect).

5 When you have created the four 'trees' make a block of each, using the block name given and the circle centre as the insertion point.

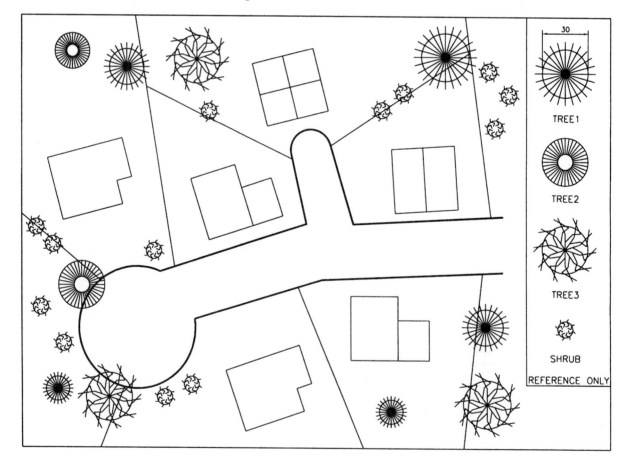

Figure 10.3 ESTATE created from the fifth menu.

6 We will now modify the menu file, so SHELL and:
EDIT C:\R13CUST\MYMENU.MNU, but note that the line numbers are for reference only and should not be entered:

a) *sub-menu*
After [HEXAGON]... enter:

   <R>
   [GREENERY]$S=TREES   line 1
   <R>
   **TREES   line 2
   [PLANTING]   line 3
   **[TREE 1]^C^C_INSERT TREE1 **   line 4
   **[TREE 2]^C^C_INSERT TREE2 **
   **[TREE 3]^C^C_INSERT TREE3 **
   **[SHRUB]^C^C_INSERT SHRUB **
   <R> 10 times   line 5
   [PREVMENU]$S=   line 6

b) *pull-down for dialogue boxes*
After [QUITING]... enter:

   ***POP5   line 7
   [BOXES]   line 8
   [AIDS...]^C^C_DDRMODES   line 9
   [LAYERS...]^C^C)_DDLMODES
   [ENTITIES...]^C^C_DDEMODES

c) *icon menu*
After [GREENERY]... enter:

   [HOUSE...]$I=HOUSES SI=*   line 10
then after [PREVMENU]... enter:
   ***IMAGE   line 11
   **HOUSES   line 12
   [House Selection]   line 13
   **[SEMI DETACHED]^C^C_INSERT SEMI **   line 14
   **[2BEDROOM FLATS]^C^C_INSERT FLAT **   line 15
   **[3BEDROOM DETACHED]^C^C_INSERT 3BED **   line 16
   **[4BEDROOM DETACHED]^C^C_INSERT 4BED **   line 17

d) File–Save As MYMENU.MNU then File–Exit.

7 At the command line enter MENU and:
a) pick Menu Template (*.MNU)
b) pick mymenu.mnu
c) pick OK
d) pick OK to menu message.

8 The drawing screen will display BOXES as an additional pull-down title and GREENERY, HOUSE... will be displayed in the screen menu area.

9 From the menu bar select **BOXES–LAYERS...** and the Layer Control dialogue box will be displayed (at long last!). Layer OUT is current, hence the red entities – but you already knew this?

10 Try the other BOXES options and cancel any resulting dialogue boxes.

11 Select GREENERY from the screen menu and you have another menu with the name PLANTING and five selections? Check that the four 'tree' selections work then pick PREVMENU which should return the main menu. You should be starting to be impressed with what has been achieved so far?

12 From the screen menu select HOUSE... and:

prompt   House Selection dialogue box which you 'programmed' as Fig. 10.4 with 'No icon!' messages

respond   pick **3BEDROOM DETACHED** and:

a) it turns blue

b) the third icon space turns black

then   pick OK and insert your house symbol full size.

13 Try the other icon selections.

14 *Question.*

a) Why are there no icon pictures of the houses?
Answer soon!

b) Pick one of the shapes SQUARE, CIRCLE or HEXAGON and an error message will be displayed. The block named ???? cannot be found in any of the directories. You should know the answer to this???

15 *Task.*

Erase any entities from the screen and using your fifth menu create a housing estate layout using Fig. 10.3 as a guide only. Let your imagination run riot with scales and rotation angles. When the drawing is complete, save it as ESTATE.

16 *Menu explanation.*

Before dealing with the 'missing icon question' we will discuss the new menu items which were numbered for reference.

line 1:   **[GREENERY]$S=TREES**

[GREENERY]: the word GREENERY is displayed in the screen menu area.

$S=TREES: 'go to' a screen sub-menu called TREES. The **$** is the sub-menu 'command' and **S** for screen.

Thus when GREENERY is selected from the screen menu, the screen sub-menu called TREES will be activated.

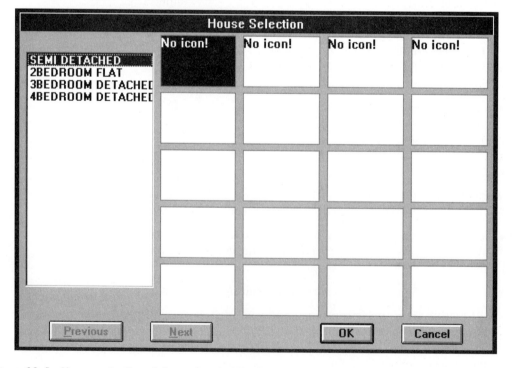

Figure 10.4   House selection dialogue box (original).

line 2: ****TREES**

**: the start of a sub-menu. Hence $S=TREES calls up the screen sub-menu TREES, which is 'loaded' with **TREES.

line 3: **[PLANTING]**

The title of the TREES sub-menu.

line 4: **[TREE 1] ^ C ^ C_INSERT TREE1 **

Display TREE 1 and when selected cancel any active command and insert the block called TREE1, waiting for user input. This is the same for the other lines in the sub-menu.

line 5: **<R>** 10 times.

This is used for blank lines in the screen menu area and will 'blank out' any text from a previous menu.

line 6: **[PREVMENU]$S=**

The $S= is used to 'load' the previous menu, hence when PREVMENU is select from the screen menu area, the main screen menu is displayed again.

line 7: *****POP5**

Indicates that a pull-down menu is to be displayed in area five.

line 8: **[BOXES]**

The title of the pull-down menu which will appear in the menu bar. This could be anything!

line 9: **[AIDS...] ^ C ^ C_DDRMODES**

Display the word AIDS... in the pull-down menu, cancel any active commands then load the dynamic dialogue (DD) box RMODES – which is the drawing aids dialogue box. Although this may seem rather complex, we are still using AutoCAD commands in our customized menu. The dialogue boxes are displayed with OK, Cancel and Help as normal. The other two pull-down commands operate in the same way with DDLMODES loading the Layer Control dialogue box and DDEMODES loading the Entity Creation dialogue box.

line 10: **[HOUSE...]$I=HOUSES $I=***

[HOUSE...]:   display HOUSE... in the screen menu area, the '...' being added to indicate that a dialogue box will follow.

$I=HOUSES: 'go to' an image sub-menu called HOUSES. The **$** is the sub-menu 'command' and **I** is used to indicate an image (icon) menu.

$I=*:   is a special AutoCAD command which must be used to display an image tile dialogue box and 'load' the appropriate slides. Thus when HOUSE... is selected from the screen, the image sub-menu called HOUSES will be activated with slide icons displayed in a dialogue box.

line 11: *****IMAGE**

Indicates that an image menu is to follow. This is the same as ***ICON on previous releases.

line 12: ****HOUSES**

**: the start of the sub-menu called HOUSES. Thus $I=HOUSES calls up the image sub-menu HOUSES which is loaded with **HOUSES.

line 13: **[House Selection]**

The title of the icon dialogue box. This can be anything.

line 14: **[SEMI DETACHED] ^ C ^ C_INSERT SEMI **

Display SEMI DETACHED in the list column and when selected cancel any active command and insert the block called SEMI waiting for user input. At the same time, display a slide in the appropriate box in the dialogue box. Selection of the slide icon will also activate the insert SEMI command. This line is the same for the other three entries.

17 *Note:* this has been a rather long explanation but I considered it essential as the fifth menu has included several new menu concepts.

18 *The missing icons.*
When the icon selection dialogue box was displayed there were no house icons – Fig. 10.4. This was because the lines 14–17 were written wrongly. I tried to be too smart with the words SEMI DETACHED, 2 BEDROOM FLATS, etc. These are wrong, as the word which is displayed in the [] brackets must be the same as the slide which was created. Our slides were named SEMI, FLAT, 3BED and 4BED (the same as the blocks) and these MUST BE the [ ] entries.

19 *Modifying the menu.*
a) SHELL-EDIT C:\R13CUST\MYMENU.MNU and alter lines 14–17 to:
**[SEMI]^C^C_INSERT SEMI **
**[FLAT]^C^C_INSERT FLAT **
**[3BED]^C^C_INSERT 3BED **
**[4BED]^C^C_INSERT 4BED **
b) File–Save As then File-Exit
c) Enter MENU at the command line and:
  i)   check directory is c:\r13cust
  ii) pick Menu Template (*.MNU)
  iii) pick mymenu.mnu then OK
  iv) pick OK to the menu message
d) Now select from the screen menu HOUSE... to display the House Selection icon dialogue box.
e) Any icons displayed? I did not have any.
f) This worried me, as I had followed the manual instructions exactly, i.e. the name in the [ ] brackets was the same as the slide name, e.g. SEMI, etc.
h) So why still no icons?
i) I managed to display icons slides in the House Selection dialogue box by using the slide library created in Chapter 8.

20 *Modifying the menu (again).*
a) SHELL-EDIT C:\R13CUST\MYMENU.MNU and alter the same lines as before to:
**[HOUSELIB(SEMI)]^C^C_INSERT SEMI **
**[HOUSELIB(FLAT)]^C^C_INSERT FLAT **
**[HOUSELIB(3BED)]^C^C_INSERT 3BED **
**[HOUSELIB(4BED)]^C^C_INSERT 4BED **
b) File–Save As and File–Exit
c) Using MENU re-select mymenu.mnu as before
d) Now select HOUSE... from the screen menu and the icons for the houses should be displayed for selection – Fig. 10.5.
e) The above lines can be read as: from the slide library named HOUSELIB, display the word SEMI in the [ ] brackets and at the same time display the slide SEMI.
f) This works, while the previous entry did not – at least it didn't work for me.

21 This completes the fifth menu. I did tell you that it would be quite complex!

22 Now you know why the slide libraries were created.

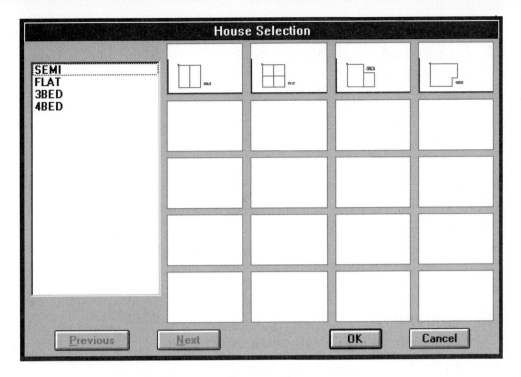

Figure 10.5 House selection dialogue box (modified).

Sixth menu: the hatch patterns in an icon menu

This menu will allow the created hatch patterns to be used from an icon menu, selected from the pull-down area.

1 Still have the ESTATE drawing on the screen similar to Fig. 10.3? If not open it.

2 Using MENU, reload acadfull.mnc – easy?

3 At the command line enter SHELL-EDIT C:\R13CUST\MYMENU.MNU and:
   a) after [DONUT]... in ***POP1 enter:
     [HATCHING...]$I=HATPATS $I=*   line 1
   b) after [HOUSELIB(4BED)]... enter:
     ****HATPATS**   line 2
     [My Own Created Hatch Patterns]   line 3
     **[HATCHLIB(TSHAPE)]^C^C_-BHATCH P TSHAPE 0.5 20 **   line 4
     **[HATCHLIB(DOUBLE)]^C^C_-BHATCH P DOUBLE 1 -30 **
     **[HATCHLIB(WEAVE)]^C^C_-BHATCH P WEAVE 2 45 **
     **[HATCHLIB(ARROW)]^C^C_-BHATCH P ARROW 0.25 0 **
     **[HATCHLIB(ARRHD)]^C^C_-BHATCH P ARRHD 1 0 **

4 File–Save As then File–Exit.

5 Re-compile the altered menu with MENU <R> then:
   a) c:\r13cust directory
   b) Menu Template (*.MNU)
   c) pick mymenu.mnu
   d) pick OK.

6 From the menu bar select **DRAWING-HATCHING...** and:

prompt   an icon dialogue box displaying My Own Created Hatch Patterns as Fig. 10.6.

respond **pick TSHAPE** from the list and:

      a) it turns blue

      b) the TSHAPE icon turns black

      c) pick OK.

prompt   `Properties....... P`

           `Scale........... 0.5`

           `Angle........... 20`

then   `Properties.....<Internal point:`

respond **pick any point in area to be hatched** then right-click.

7 The selected area will be hatched with the TSHAPE pattern at a scale of 0.5 and angle of 20 as entered in our menu.

8 Using the hatch patterns from the icon dialogue box, complete the estate drawing similar to Fig. 10.7. Note that you will have to add some extra lines, etc.

9 When complete, save as ESTATE.

Sixth menu notes

The new additions to our customized menu are:

line 1:   **[HATCHING...]$I=HATPATS $I=***

           [HATCHING...]: display HATCHING... in the pull-down area DRAWING after DONUT

           $I=HATPATS: the name of an icon sub-menu

           $I=*: the special command to display image tiles

           Thus when HATCHING... is selected, load the icon sub-menu named HATPATS in an image dialogue box form.

line 2:   ****HATPATS**

           The name and start of the icon sub-menu from $I=HATPATS

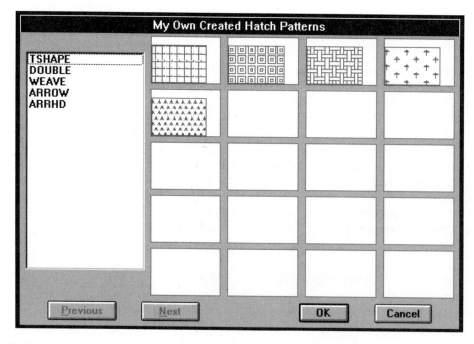

Figure 10.6 Created hatch patterns dialogue box.

line 3: **[My Own Created Hatch Patterns]**
The title to be displayed in the icon pop-up menu. This can be anything.

line 4: **[HATCHLIB(TSHAPE)] ^ C ^ C_-BHATCH P TSHAPE 0.5 20 **
The line which makes it all happen!

[HATCHLIB(TSHAPE)]: from the slide library named HATCHLIB, display the word TSHAPE in the list column and display the slide TSHAPE as an icon in the first box.

^ C ^ C_: cancel any active command and remember (_) is a spacer.

-BHATCH: the boundary hatch command used in a slightly different manner. The (-) before BHATCH indicates that the BHATCH dialogue box is *not to be used*.

P: the properties option of the BHATCH command which allows the hatch name to be entered.

TSHAPE: the name of the hatch pattern to be used.

0.5: the scale of the TSHAPE pattern.

20: the angle of the hatch pattern.

\: a pause for user input.

This line can thus be read as:

Display TSHAPE in the icon list column and display the slide in the icon box. When TSHAPE is selected from the list or icon, cancel any active command and activate the BHATCH command with command line entry. Select the TSHAPE hatch pattern, set the pattern scale to 0.5 and the angle to 20 and await user selection of an internal point which is to be hatched.

11 This completes the sixth menu exercise.

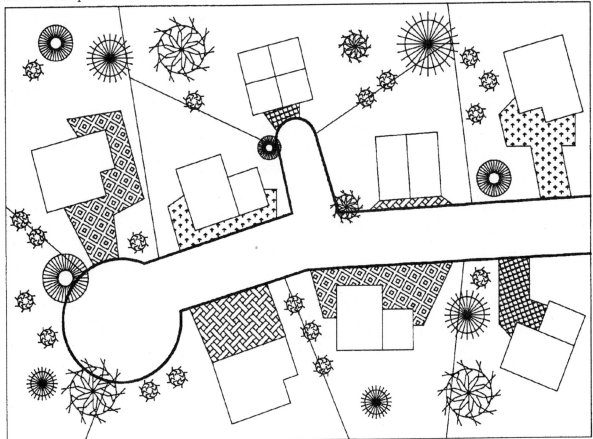

Figure 10.7 ESTATE created from the sixth menu.

Seventh menu: a customized toolbar

In this section we will customize a toolbar with our own icons so:

1 Open your STDA3 standard sheet with acadfull.mnc.

2 Refer to Fig. 10.8 then select **Tools**
Customize Toolbars...

prompt	`Toolbars` dialogue box
respond	pick **New...**
prompt	`New Toolbar` dialogue box
respond	*a*) enter **MINE** as the Toolbar Name
	b) pick OK.
prompt	`Toolbars` dialogue box
respond	pick **Close**.

3 A new toolbar will be displayed on the screen as fig. (a). At present it does not contain any icons but it can be moved in the usual manner. I would suggest that you move it as far to the right as possible, without it becoming docked.

4 From the menu bar select **Tools–Customize Toolbars** and:

prompt	`Toolbars` dialogue box
respond	pick **Customize...**
prompt	Customize Toolbars dialogue box
respond	*a*) scroll at Categories
	b) pick **Standard**
prompt	`Customize` dialogue box with the Standard icons displayed
respond	*a*) left-click on the REDRAW icon and hold down the left button
	b) drag the icon into the new toolbar area
	c) release the left button
	d) the REDRAW icon will be displayed in the new toolbar – fig. (b).
	e) left-click on the UNDO icon and hold down
	f) drag the icon into the new toolbar
	g) release the left button – fig. (c)
	h) *i*) pick Close to exit the Customize dialogue box
	ii) pick Close to exit the Toolbars dialogue box.

5 Using step four add the REDO and REDRAW ALL icons from the Standard category – fig. (d).

6 Select Tools–Customize Toolbars and:
a) scroll at Categories and pick Miscellaneous
b) move the OOPS icon into the new toolbar – fig. (e)
c) Close and Close.

7 You can now add other icons of your choice.

8 The new toolbar cannot (as yet) be used with our customized menu and can only be used with the acad menus. When our menu has been altered, it must be re-compiled and the message (Fig. 10.1) is always displayed:

"Loading the template menu file overwrites and redefines the menu source file, which results in the loss of any toolbar customized changes that have been made".

Think what this means!

9 The new toolbar can be cancelled as normal and can re-displayed by entering at the command line **TOOLBAR** <R> and:

prompt   Toolbar name (or ALL)
enter   **MINE** <R>
prompt   Show..... <Show>
respond   right-click.

10 The new toolbar will be displayed and can be docked or positioned to suit.

11 The options allow the toolbar being displayed to be docked at the Left, Right, etc.

12 This completes our customized toolbar exercise.

(a)New toolbar created.

(b)REDRAW icon added

(c)UNDO icon added.

(d)REDO and REDRAW ALL icons.

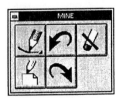

(e)OOPS icon added.

Figure 10.8 Toolbar customization.

Eighth menu (and last): a tablet menu

This menu can only be used if you use (or have access to) a digitizing tablet compatible with AutoCAD. The menu requires a puck as the pointing device and will not work with the mouse. If you do not have access to a tablet then forget this exercise completely. The menu will insert created blocks by selection from the tablet.

Creating the blocks

1 Open your STDA3 standard sheet and refer to Fig. 10.9.

2 Draw the nine objects using the sizes given.

3 Make blocks of each object with:
   a) the name given as the block name
   b) the insertion point at the top-left of the object – this is a suggestion only
   c) DO NOT ADD DIMENSIONS.

4 At this point save your drawing as C:\R13CUST\KITCHEN.

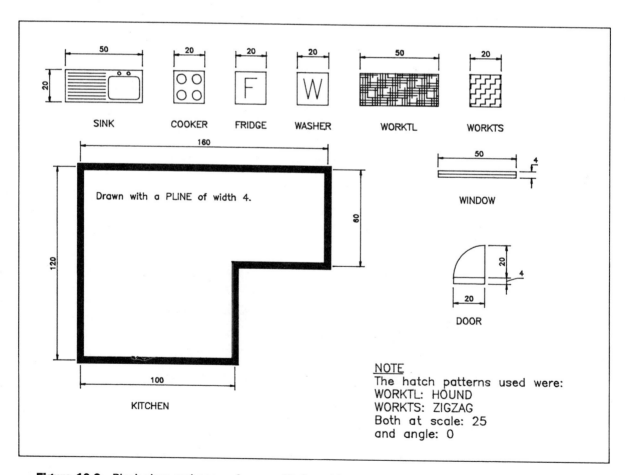

Figure 10.9 Block sizes and names for use with the tablet menu.

Modifying the menu

1 At the command line enter **SHELL-EDIT C:\r13CUST\MYMENU.MNU** and:

a) after [HOUSE...] enter:

<R>	line 1
[TABLET]$S=TABLET	line 2

b) after [PREVMENU]$S= enter:

<R>	
**TABLET	line 3
***SCREEN	line 4
<R> 20 times line 5	
[PREVMENU]$S=	line 6
<R>	
***TABLET1	line 7
**^C^C_INSERT SINK **	line 8
**^C^C_INSERT COOKER **	
**^C^C_INSERT FRIDGE **	
**^C^C_INSERT WASHER **	
**^C^C_INSERT WORKTL **	
**^C^C_INSERT WORKTS **	
**^C^C_INSERT DOOR **	
**^C^C_INSERT WINDOW **	
**^C^C_INSERT KITCHEN **	
***TABLET2	line 9
^C^C_COPY	
^C^C_MOVE	
^C^C_ROTATE	
^C^C_MIRROR	
^C^C_LINE	
^C^C_DTEXT	
^C^C_ERASE	
'REDRAW	line 10
'REDRAW	line 11

2 File–Save As then File–Exit.

3 Using MENU and Menu Template, select mymenu.mnu.

4 The screen menu should display TABLET.

Configuring the tablet

1 Cut out the tablet overlay (Fig. 10.10) and fix it to your tablet which consists of a screen menu area and two menu areas. The kitchen symbols are in menu area one and some commands are in menu area two. Each menu area consists of one column and several rows. The order of the symbols in menu area one is the same as the line menu order and this is essential in tablet menus.

2 From the menu bar select **Options**
                            Tablet
                            Configure

prompt	Enter number of tablet menus desired (0-4)
enter	**2** <R>
prompt	Digitize upper left corner of menu area 1
respond	pick **pt1**
prompt	Digitize lower left corner of menu area 1
respond	pick **pt2**
prompt	Digitize lower right corner of menu area 1
respond	pick **pt3**
prompt	Enter the number of columns for menu area 1
enter	**1** <R>
prompt	Enter the number of rows for menu area 1
enter	**9** <R>
prompt	Digitize upper left corner of menu area 2
respond	pick **pt4**
prompt	Digitize lower left corner of menu area 2
respond	pick **pt5**
prompt	Digitize lower left corner of menu area 2
respond	pick **pt6**
prompt	Enter the number of columns for menu area 2
enter	**1** <R>
prompt	Enter the number of rows for menu area 2
enter	**9** <R>
prompt	Do you want to respecify the Fixed Screen pointing area?
enter	**Y** <R>
prompt	Digitize lower left corner of Fixed Screen pointing area
respond	pick **pt7**
prompt	Digitize upper right corner of Fixed Screen pointing area
respond	pick **pt8**
prompt	Do you want to specify the Floating Screen pointing area?
enter	**N** <R>

Using the tablet

1 From the screen menu select TABLET and only PREVMENU will be displayed.

2 Refer to Fig. 10.11 and use the tablet menu to construct a kitchen layout of your own design.
Note: I used a snap of 2 for this – why 2?

3 Save your drawing when it is complete.

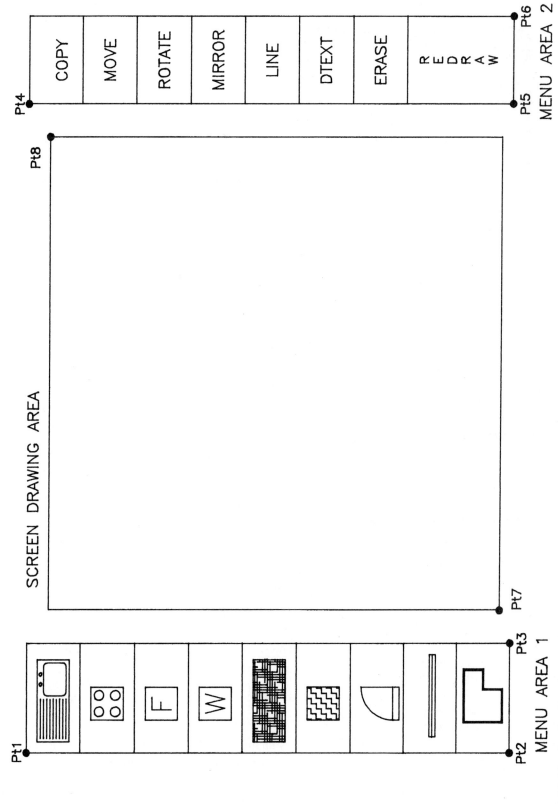

Figure 10.10 Overlay for use with the tablet menu.

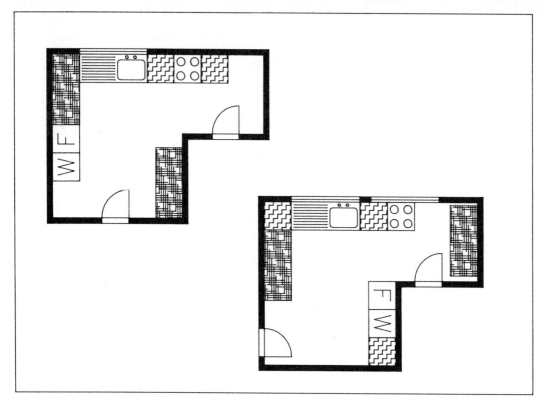

Figure 10.11 Kitchen layouts using the tablet menu.

New item explanation

The new menu items have included:

line 1: **<R>**

To give a blank line after [HOUSE...]

line 2: **[TABLET]$S=TABLET**

Display the ward TABLET in the screen menu area, and when selected, activate the sub-menu called TABLET

line 3: ****TABLET**

The start of the sub-menu called TABLET, 'called up' from $S=TABLET

line 4: *****SCREEN**

Within the sub-menu called TABLET there will be a screen menu.

line 5: **<R> twenty times**

Display 20 blank lines in the screen menu area. This is to 'blank out' any items which exist in this area.

line 6: **[PREVMENU]$S=**

The only item displayed in the menu area to allow a return to the main screen menu when selected.

line 7: *****TABLET1**

Start of tablet menu area one and is included in the sub-menu TABLET. The items which follow must be in the same order as the items in menu area one on the tablet overlay.

line 8: **^C^C_INSERT SINK **

Insert the created block SINK when the first item in menu area one is selected from the tablet overlay.

line 9:   *****TABLET2**
Start of tablet menu area two and the items which follow must be in the same order as the items in menu area two of the tablet overlay.

line 10:   **'REDRAW**
Activate the transparent REDRAW command when selected.

line 11:   **'REDRAW**
The REDRAW command is entered twice in the menu as the item 'covers two boxes' in the tablet menu.

And now...

This completes the menu exercises for this chapter. I have imported the complete C:\R13CUST\MYMENU.MNU menu file into a drawing for reference – Fig. 10.12.

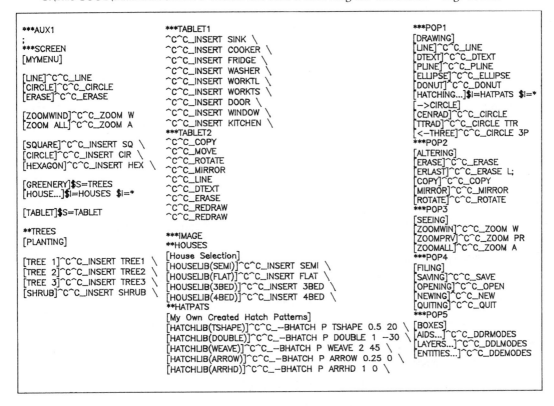

```
***AUX1                    ***TABLET1                              ***POP1
;                          ^C^C_INSERT SINK \                     [DRAWING]
***SCREEN                  ^C^C_INSERT COOKER \                   [LINE]^C^C_LINE
[MYMENU]                   ^C^C_INSERT FRIDGE \                   [DTEXT]^C^C_DTEXT
                           ^C^C_INSERT WASHER \                   [PLINE]^C^C_PLINE
[LINE]^C^C_LINE            ^C^C_INSERT WORKTL \                   [ELLIPSE]^C^C_ELLIPSE
[CIRCLE]^C^C_CIRCLE        ^C^C_INSERT WORKTS \                   [DONUT]^C^C_DONUT
[ERASE]^C^C_ERASE          ^C^C_INSERT DOOR \                     [HATCHING...]$I=HATPATS $I=*
                           ^C^C_INSERT WINDOW \                   [->CIRCLE]
[ZOOMWIND]^C^C_ZOOM W      ^C^C_INSERT KITCHEN \                  [CENRAD]^C^C_CIRCLE
[ZOOM ALL]^C^C_ZOOM A      ***TABLET2                             [TTRAD]^C^C_CIRCLE TTR
                           ^C^C_COPY                              [<-THREE]^C^C_CIRCLE 3P
[SQUARE]^C^C_INSERT SQ \   ^C^C_MOVE                              ***POP2
[CIRCLE]^C^C_INSERT CIR \  ^C^C_ROTATE                            [ALTERING]
[HEXAGON]^C^C_INSERT HEX \ ^C^C_MIRROR                            [ERASE]^C^C_ERASE
                           ^C^C_LINE                              [ERLAST]^C^C_ERASE L;
[GREENERY]$S=TREES         ^C^C_DTEXT                             [COPY]^C^C_COPY
[HOUSE...]$I=HOUSES $I=*   ^C^C_ERASE                             [MIRROR]^C^C_MIRROR
                           ^C^C_REDRAW                            [ROTATE]^C^C_ROTATE
[TABLET]$S=TABLET          ^C^C_REDRAW                            ***POP3
                                                                  [SEEING]
**TREES                                                           [ZOOMWIN]^C^C_ZOOM W
[PLANTING]                 ***IMAGE                               [ZOOMPRV]^C^C_ZOOM PR
                           **HOUSES                               [ZOOMALL]^C^C_ZOOM A
[TREE 1]^C^C_INSERT TREE1 \ [House Selection]                     ***POP4
[TREE 2]^C^C_INSERT TREE2 \ [HOUSELIB(SEMI)]^C^C_INSERT SEMI \    [FILING]
[TREE 3]^C^C_INSERT TREE3 \ [HOUSELIB(FLAT)]^C^C_INSERT FLAT \    [SAVING]^C^C_SAVE
[SHRUB]^C^C_INSERT SHRUB \ [HOUSELIB(3BED)]^C^C_INSERT 3BED \     [OPENING]^C^C_OPEN
                           [HOUSELIB(4BED)]^C^C_INSERT 4BED \     [NEWING]^C^C_NEW
                           **HATPATS                              [QUITING]^C^C_QUIT
                           [My Own Created Hatch Patterns]        ***POP5
                           [HATCHLIB(TSHAPE)]^C^C_-BHATCH P TSHAPE 0.5 20 \   [BOXES]
                           [HATCHLIB(DOUBLE)]^C^C_-BHATCH P DOUBLE 1 -30 \    [AIDS...]^C^C_DDRMODES
                           [HATCHLIB(WEAVE)]^C^C_-BHATCH P WEAVE 2 45 \       [LAYERS...]^C^C_DDLMODES
                           [HATCHLIB(ARROW)]^C^C_-BHATCH P ARROW 0.25 0 \     [ENTITIES...]^C^C_DDEMODES
                           [HATCHLIB(ARRHD)]^C^C_-BHATCH P ARRHD 1 0 \
```

Figure 10.12 Complte listing of C:\R13CUST\MYMENU.MNU.

Summary

1 Menu files are text files written by the user. All user-written text files have the extension **.MNU**

2 The main AutoCAD menu files are:
   a) c:\r13\win\support\acad.mnu – the short menu
   b) c:\r13\win\support\acadfull.mnu – the full menu. These file names should be noted for reference.

3 AutoCAD menu file extensions are:
   .MNU: template menu file
   .MNC: compiled menu file
   .MNR: menu resource file
   .MNS: source menu file.

4 Menu files are identified with section labels as follows:

section label	menu area
***SCREEN	screen menu area
***POPn	pull-down menu area (0–16)
***IMAGE	image tile menu area
***AUXn	auxiliary menu (1–4)
***BUTTONSn	pointing device menu (1–4)
***TABLETn	tablet menu area (1–4)

5 Menu syntax is determined by special characters, and the following table lists the most common items:

character	usage
***	section title
**	sub-menu section label
[ ]	label for screen, pull-down, icon and slide menus
;	equivalent to a <RETURN>
$	loads a menu section (e.g. sub-menu)
^C^C	cancels any active command
_	translates AutoCAD commands that follow
\	pause for user input.

6 Slides can be included in image tile menus, but a slide library must exist containing the slides.

7 Tablet menus are usually used with pre-created blocks.

Activity

Creating menus can be interesting or boring depending on how good you are with them. I have included a menu activity, which is quite demanding and time-consuming. It will certainly test your ability and patience.

1 Refer to Tutorial 8(a) and create the components to the sizes given. Drawing the components with the snap on (5 setting) will help when the blocks are being inserted.

2 Create blocks of each component using the block name and suggested insertion point.

3 As an added interest add an attribute definition to the resistor which will assist with the text values when the block is being inserted.

4 Write a new menu called **SCMEN.MNU** which will allow all the blocks to be inserted into a drawing. Use the pull-down menus as follows:

```
***POP1    ***POP2
[BLOCKS]    [COMMANDS]
RES         LINE
NPN         ERASE
etc., etc.  etc., etc.
```

5 Use your new menu to complete the electrical circuit layout displayed in Tutorial 8(b). *Note*: if this drawing is completed 'full size' you will need to increase the limits and zoom-all, etc. I have scaled the complete circuit to fit A3 paper for printing reasons.

6 If you are feeling really adventurous, you could try and write a tablet menu for completing the layout. The tablet menu would be virtually identical to our worked example, the electrical blocks replacing the kitchen blocks in the overlay and menu.

Chapter 11

Data exchange

Transferring data from CAD is always one of the justifications for the expense of installing a CAD system. This transfer may be to other CAD systems, for CNC machining, database transactions, spreadsheet usage, etc. In an earlier chapter, we created attribute extraction files and extracted TEXT information in CDF and SDF formats. In this chapter we will investigate several methods of transferring **DRAWING** information in/out of AutoCAD.

Release 13 supports many different file formats including:

Format	Export	Import
Windows Metafile (WMF)	✔	✔
ACIS (SAT)	✔	✔
PostScript (EPS)	✔	✔
Bitmap (BMP)	✔	✘
Drawing Interchange (DXF)	✔	✔
3D Studio (3DS)	✔	✔
Paint (PCX)	✔	✘
TIFF (TIF)	✔	✔
GIF (GIF)	✔	✔

Release 13 does NOT support the Initial Graphics Exchange Specification (IGES) format.

The drawing

1 Open your STDA3 standard sheet.

2 Refer to Fig. 11.1 and draw the component as shown. Add the text and all dimensions and use layers correctly, i.e. OUT, CL, DIM, etc. Position the circle centres at the point 100,120.

3 Erase the border and any other entities to leave the drawing, text item and dimensions.

4 Save the drawing as **C:\R13CUST\COUPLING**.

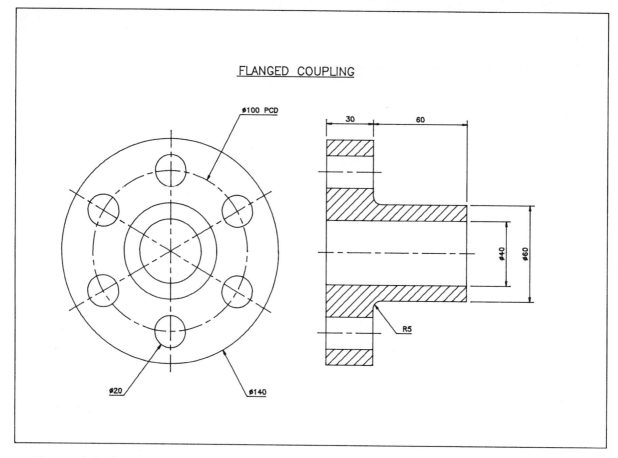

Figure 11.1 Component for use with data exchange examples.

Exporting data

To demonstrate how files are exported in different formats, we will use the drawing of the flanged coupling.

Creating a DXF file

Drawing Interchange Format (DXF) files can be read by other CAD systems and most CNC systems.

1 Open your C:\R13CUST\COUPLING drawing.

2 At the command line enter **DXFOUT** <R> and:
  prompt   Create DXF dialogue box
  respond   *a*) check directory c:\r13cust
        b) check file name coupling
        c) pick OK
  prompt   Enter decimal places.....
  enter   **6** <R>

3 The command line is returned.

4 Repeat the DXFOUT command and:

    prompt   Create DXF dialogue box

    respond   *a*) alter file name to **coupl_1**

               b) pick OK

    prompt   Enter decimal places.....

    enter   **O** <R> – the objects option

    prompt   Select objects

    respond **window the left view** (excluding dimensions)

    prompt   ?? found

    respond right-click

    prompt   Enter decimal places.....

    enter   **6** <R>.

5 We have created two DXF output files:

    a) COUPLING: the complete drawing

    b) COUPL_1: the left view.

6 *Note.*

    a) the extension **.dxf** is automatically added to the file name

    b) do not confuse the extensions .dxf and .dxx

      .dxf: is the extension for a DXF **drawing** output file

      .dxx: is an attribute (**text**) extraction file extension.

Creating a WMF file

Window Metafile Format (WMF) files are very good representations of drawings as they contain screen vectors and raster graphics. The procedure for creating a WMF file is very straightforward so:

1 Open the COUPLING drawing.

2 At the command line enter **WMFOUT** <R> and:

    prompt   Create WMF dialogue box

    respond   *a*) directory c:\r13cust

               b) file name coupling

               c) pick OK

    prompt   Select objects

    respond window the complete drawing then right-click.

3 The extension .wmf is added to the file name.

Creating a Bitmap file

Bitmap (BMP) files are very suited to Windows graphic packages and are very easy to create.

1 Open the COUPLING drawing.

2 At the command line enter **BMPOUT** and:

    prompt   Create BMP file dialogue box

    respond   *a*) directory c:r13cust

               b) file name coupling

               c) pick OK

    prompt   Select objects

    respond window the drawing then right-click.

3 The bitmap file is created as coupling.bmp.

Creating a PostScript file

PostScript files are graphical files particularly suited to electronic publishing work, and PostScript fonts can be used in AutoCAD to enhance the AutoCAD text fonts. PostScript files have the extension (**.EPS**) which is an abbreviation for encapsulated PostScript.

1 Open the COUPLING drawing.
2 At the command line enter **PSOUT** and:

prompt   Create Postscript dialogue box
respond *a*) directory c:\r13cust
          b) filename coupling
          c) pick OK
prompt   What to plot.....
enter   **D** <R> – the display option
prompt   Include a screen preview image.....
enter   **E** <R> – the EPSI option
prompt   Screen preview image size.....
respond <R> – accept the 128 default
prompt   Size units.....
enter   **M** <R> – for millimetres
prompt   Output Millimetres.....
enter   **F** <R> – the fit option
prompt   Text screen with: Standard values for output size
enter   **A3** <R>
prompt   Effective plotting area 273.00 wide by 129.02 high.

3 The command line is returned and the extension .EPS is added to the output file.

Raster screen export files

Raster files create an image of the drawing screen which can be used in software packages where accuracy is not of the greatest importance, e.g. in animation, logo design, etc. Two commonly used raster formats are:

GIF: Graphics Interchange Format
TIFF: Tag Image File Format

The sequence of creating GIF and TIFF files is similar to creating a plot file with several prompts and user responses. Many of these prompts will probably mean nothing to you, but the exercises are worthwhile completing as the end result can be interesting.

Creating a raster GIF file

1 Open your COUPLING drawing.

2 From the menu bar select **Options–Configure**

prompt	Text screen with a list of the supported devices, i.e. video display, digitizer, plotter
respond	<RETURN>
prompt	Configure Menu options 0-7
enter	**5** <R> – plotter configuration
prompt	Plotter Configure Menu
enter	**1** <R> – add plotter option
prompt	Available plotter list
enter	**14** <R> – raster file export
prompt	Supported model list
enter	**5** <R> – for VGA
prompt	Raster file format list
enter	**1** <R> – for GIF format
prompt	GIF message
then	Interlace output lines?
enter	**N** <R>
prompt	Colour image option
enter	**3** <R>
prompt	background colour option
enter	**7** <R> for white or **0** <R> for black
prompt	Sizes are in Inches and the style is landscape
	Plot origin is at (0.00, 0.00)
	Plotting area is 640 wide and 480 high (MAX size)
	Plot is NOT rotated
	Hidden lines will NOT be removed
	Plot will be scaled to fit available area
then	Do you want to change anything?
enter	**Y** <R>
prompt	Standard colour list
enter	**N** <R> – for no change
prompt	Calibrate plotter?
enter	**N** <R> – we are NOT using the plotter
prompt	Size units
enter	**M** <R> – for millimetres
prompt	Plot origin
enter	**0,0** <R>
prompt	Standard values for plotting sizes
enter	**A3** <R> – our standard sheet size
prompt	Rotate plot and enter **0** <R>
prompt	Remove hidden lines and enter **N** <R>
prompt	Plotted units and enter **F** <R>
prompt	Enter a description of this plotter
enter	**GIFTEST** <R>
prompt	Plotter Configure Menu
enter	**0** <R> – to exit
prompt	Configure Menu
enter	**0** <R> – to exit
prompt	Keep configuration changes?
enter	**Y** <R>
prompt	The command line is returned.

3 The above sequence seems to have achieved absolutely nothing, but we have set an output configuration to GIF format.

4 From the menu bar select **File**
> **Print...**

prompt   Plot Configuration dialogue box
respond pick **Device and Default Selection...**
prompt   Device and Default Selection dialogue box
respond *a*) pick **GIFTEST** and it turns blue
           b) pick OK
prompt   Device and Default Selection dialogue box
respond pick **File Name...**
prompt   Create Plot File dialogue box
respond *a*) check directory c:\r13cust
           b) enter file name **COUPLING.GIF**
           c) pick OK
           d) pick OK from Plot Configuration dialogue box
prompt   Effective plotting area 396 wide by 187.15 high
           Vector sort done 100%
           Plot complete.

5 Again nothing seems to have happened, but we have created a plot file of the coupling drawing in GIF format.

Creating a raster TIFF file

The method of creating this file format is identical to the GIF procedure and the prompts/responses will be given as a listed sequence so:

1 Open the COUPLING drawing.

2 From the menu bar select **Options–Configure** and respond:

<R>	to configure screen
5	configure plotter
1	add a plotter configuration
14	raster file export
5	640×480 (VGA)
10	TIFF format
N	for compression
3	all colours
0/7	black/white background
Y	for changes
N	leave standard colours
N	no plotter calibration
M	millimetres
0,0	plot origin
A3	standard size
0	no rotation
N	no hidden line removal
F	plot to be fitted
TIFFTEST	description of plotter
0	exit Plotter Configuration Menu
0	exit Configuration Menu
Y	keep changes.

3 From the menu bar select **File–Print...** and respond:

Device and Default...	pick box
TIFFTEST	pick name from list then OK
File Name...	pick box
directory	check c:\r13cust
File Name	enter **COUPLING.TIF** then OK
pick OK.	

4 Again nothing seems to have happened, but we have created a plot file called COUPLING.TIF.

Other export formats

Release 13 also allows the following export files to be created:

1 ACIS: used for solid models and regions. The command is ACISOUT.

2 3D Studio: AutoCAD geometry and rendering can be used as input to the 3D studio package. The command is 3DSOUT.

These two export formats will not be discussed in this book.

Checking the created files

We have now created several export files and will now check that they are stored in our named directory so:

1 At the command line enter **SHELL** <R> and:

prompt	OS Command
enter	**<RETURN>**
prompt	DOS screen with current directory name C:\R13\WIN – my current directory
enter	**DIR C:\R13CUST\COUPLING.*** <R>
prompt	listing of COUPLING files:

```
COUPLING GIF      844
COUPLING DXF   57,566
COUPLING DWG   38,092
COUPLING BMP   11,790
COUPLING WMF    8,374
COUPLING EPS   17,774
COUPLING TIF    1,990
```

2 Study the file listing and note that a COUPLING file exists for every created file format. The various formats use different amounts of memory, with the DXF format being the largest. The basic COUPLING drawing (.DWG) uses 38,092 bytes of memory which is quite large considering the simple nature of the drawing.
Question: any idea why the DXF file is so large?

3 Return to the drawing screen by entering **EXIT** <R> at the prompt line.

Importing data

Now that we have created several file formats for our coupling drawing, we will now investigate how these files can be imported into AutoCAD. This may seem to be a bit stupid as we have the original COUPLING drawing, but it will be interesting to 'see' if the imported file types display the drawing correctly.

Importing a DXF file

1 Begin a NEW drawing and accept the default drawing name.

2 At the command line enter **DXFIN** <R> and:
  prompt   Select DXF File dialogue box
  respond   *a*) change directory to **c:\r13cust**
        b) pick file **coupling.dxf**
        c) pick OK.

3 The coupling 'drawing' should be displayed with text and dimensions.

4 Check: *a*) circle centres at 100,120?
        b) all layers available?
        c) individual entities can be erased?

5 It's as easy as that! – or is it?

Importing a WMF file

1 Begin a new drawing and accept the default name.

2 At the command line enter **WMFIN** <R> and:
  prompt   Import WMF dialogue box
  respond   *a*) change directory to c:\r13cust
        b) pick file name **coupling.wmf**
        c) pick OK
  prompt   Insertion point – note drag effect
  enter   **0,290** <R>
  prompt   X scale... and enter **1** <R>
  prompt   Y scale... and enter **1** <R>
  prompt   Rotation... and enter **0** <R>.

3 The coupling 'drawing' will be displayed.

4 *Questions.*
  a) why not (0,0) as the insertion point?
  b) is the coupling a drawing or a block?
  c) can it be exploded?
  d) have the layers been imported?

5 When importing a WMF file there are two options which can be set by the user which influence filled entities. These options are activated by selecting from the menu bar **File**
    Option
    WMF Options...
  a) Wire Frame (No Fill)
    ON (X in box):   objects imported without fill.
    OFF (no X):   objects imported filled.

b) Wide Lines
  ON (X in box):   imported polylines as drawn.
  OFF (no X):   lines imported with zero width.

Importing BMP files

AutoCAD Release 13 has no command to import a file with a BMP extension.

Importing an EPS file

Encapsulated postscript files (EPS) can be imported into AutoCAD and the user can 'set' the quality of display required.

1 Begin a new drawing accepting the default name and refer to Fig. 11.2.
2 From the menu bar select **File**
                                Option
                                PostScript Display
prompt   PSIN drag mode <0>
enter   **1** <R>

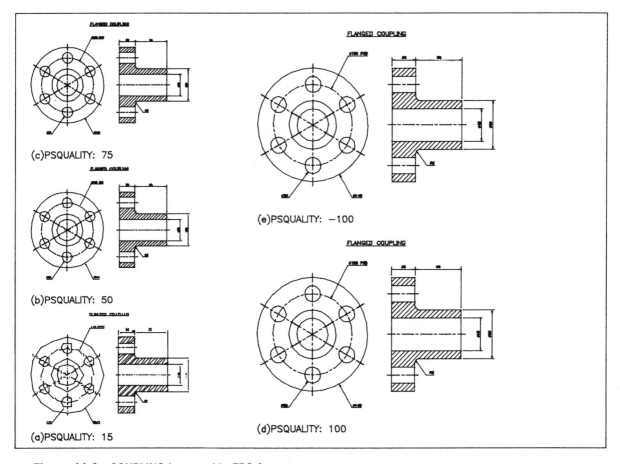

Figure 11.2 COUPLING imported in EPS format.

3 From the menu bar select **File**

                                Options

                                PostScript Quality

prompt   PSQUALITY <75?>
enter   **15** <R>

4 At the command line enter **PSIN** <R> and:
prompt   Select PS File dialogue box
respond   *a*) directory c:\r13cust
            b) file name **coupling.eps**
            c) pick OK
prompt   ....
then   Insertion point <0,0,0>
enter   **0,0** <R>
and   'ghost image' of coupling
prompt   Scale factor
enter   **100** <R>

5 The coupling EPS file is displayed – fig. (a).

6 *Questions.*
   a) is the imported file a single entity?
   b) does it explode?
   c) any layers imported?

7 At the command line enter **PSQUALITY** <R> and:
prompt   New value for PSQUALITY <15>
enter   **50** <R>.

8 Enter **PSIN** <R> and:
   a) pick coupling.eps file
   b) enter **0,90** as the insertion point
   c) enter **100** as the scale factor – fig. (b).

9 Change the PSQUALITY variable to 75, and use PSIN with:
   a) coupling.eps
   b) **0,180** as the insertion point
   c) **100** as the scale factor – fig. (c).

10 Change the PSQUALITY variable again to 100 and import the coupling.eps file:
   a) at **140,10**
   b) with a scale factor of **150** – fig. (d).

11 Finally change PSQUALITY to **–100** and import the coupling.eps file:
   a) at **140,140**
   b) at **150** scale factor – fig. (e).

12 Note the effect of the PSQUALITY system variable on:
   a) the imported display as the value increases
   b) the fill effect (+ve value) and the unfill effect (–ve value).

Importing GIF and TIF files

These two formats are identical in operation and give the same result for the same exported drawing.

1 Begin a new drawing and accept the default name.

2 At the command line enter **GIFIN** <R> and:

prompt	`Initializing...`
then	`GIF file name`
enter	**C:\R13CUST\COUPLING** <R>
prompt	`Insertion point <0,0,0>`
enter	**10,20** <R>
prompt	`Scale factor`
enter	**200** <R>.

3 At the command line enter **TIFFIN** <R> and:

prompt	`TIFF file name`
enter	**C:\R13CUST\COUPLING** <R>
prompt	`Insertion point <0,0,0>`
enter	**180,120** <R>
prompt	`Scale factor and enter` **200** <R>**.**

4 The GIF and TIF imported files are not as you expected? The screen probably displays some red, green, blue, magenta coloured squares and rectangles but it does not resemble the coupling drawing from which the export files were created. I have included my two import files – Fig. 11.3.

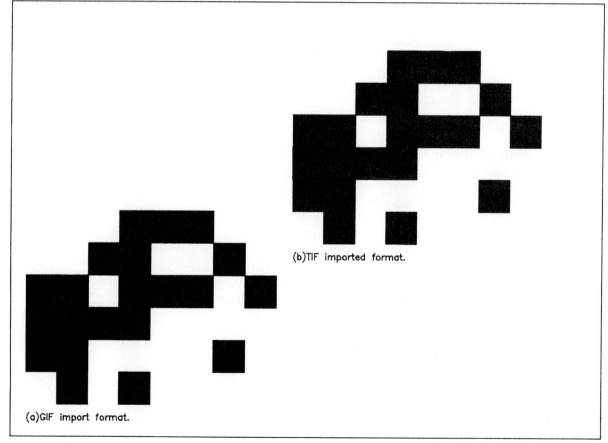

(b)TIF imported format.

(a)GIF import format.

Figure 11.3 COUPLING as GIF and TIFF imported files.

Using other software packages with AutoCAD

It is very difficult for me to demonstrate how exported AutoCAD files can be used with other software packages, as I have no idea of the packages on your system. There is one package to which every user should have access, **PAINTBRUSH** – a Windows graphics application. I will assume that this is loaded on your system and we will investigate how to 'switch' between AutoCAD and Paintbrush.

1 Open your COUPLING drawing and:
  a) de-activate ALL toolbars
  b) ensure the grid is OFF
  c) move the complete drawing from 100,120 by @0,50
  d) movc the cross-hairs 'outwith' the drawing.

2 Press the **Print Scrn** key on your keyboard.

3 Left-click on the top left window icon to display the window pull-down menu as Fig. 11.4

4 Left-click on **Switch To...** to display the Task List dialogue box as Fig. 11.5.

5 Double left-click on Program Manager to display your Windows screen.

6 From Accessories double left-click on the Paintbrush icon to display the general paintbrush screen.

7 Maximize this screen.

8 From the menu bar select **Edit–Paste** to display the coupling drawing from AutoCAD.

9 Use some of the Paintbrush draw options to add some other items to the coupling drawing.

10 When enough objects have been added select from the menu bar **File–Save As...** and:
  prompt   Save As dialogue box
  respond   *a*) change directory to **c:\r13cust**
          b) change file type to ***.PCX**
          c) enter file name **coupling**
          d) pick OK.

11 Return to AutoCAD with:
  a) left-click on top left window icon
  b) pick Close
  c) left-click on top left windows icon
  d) pick Switch To...
  e) double left-click on AutoCAD [COUPLING.DWG].

12 You will be returned to your original drawing.

13 *Note*: the procedure for switching from AutoCAD to other Windows packages is very useful and relatively easy once you get the basic idea described above. We will use this process in the next chapter.

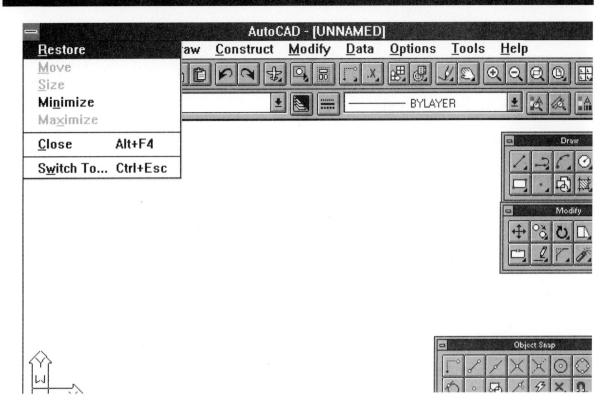

Figure 11.4 Pull-down and Switch To.

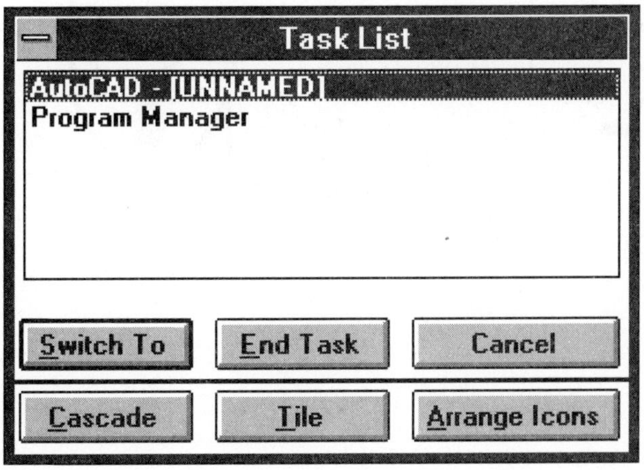

Figure 11.5 Task list dialogue box.

Importing a PCX file

To import the created PCX file from Paintbrush:

1 Begin a new drawing accepting the default name.

2 At the command line enter **PCXIN** <R> and:

prompt	PCX file name
enter	**C:\R13CUST\COUPLING**
prompt	Insertion point <0,0,0>
enter	**10,10** <R>
prompt	Scale factor and enter **250** <R>.

3 Figure 11.6 displays my coupling.pcx import file.

4 The drawing image is not very good, but is it useful?

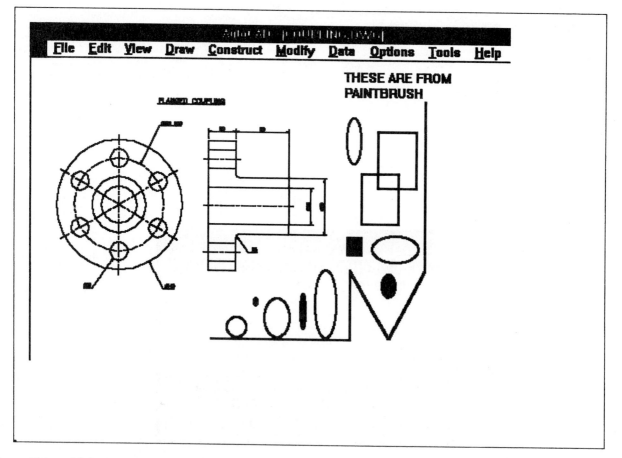

Figure 11.6 Imported PCX file from Paintbrush.

Importing text files

Most users will probably know how to import text files into an AutoCAD drawing. To complete the chapter on importing we will create a text file (which will also be used in the next chapter) and then import it into an existing drawing. If you know the process it will do you no harm to complete the exercise.

1 Open your COUPLING drawing.

2 At the command line enter **SHELL** <R> and:
   prompt   OS Command
   enter   **EDIT C:\R13CUST\REPORT_1.TXT** <R>
   prompt   MS DOS Text editor
   respond   enter the following text lines:
             TECHNICAL REPORT ACAD/R13/RMF/12-45/DF <R>
             <R>
             This report is an introduction to the work for the<R>
             JAMBOLY OIL COMPANY of MONYIA. This company is one<R>
             of our most valued customers, and it is essential<R>
             that everything that can be done for them is carried<R>
             out efficiently and correctly.<R>
   then   File–Save As and File–Exit to return to drawing.

3 Select the Text icon from the Draw toolbar and:
   prompt   Attach/.....
   enter   **H** <R> – the height option
   prompt   Height <?> and enter **4** <R>
   prompt   Attach/...../<Insertion point>
   enter   **15,255** <R>
   prompt   Attach/...../<Other corner>
   enter   **300,170** <R>
   prompt   perhaps a Select Font message?
   respond   pick **Cancel**
   prompt   Edit MText dialogue box
   respond   pick **Import...**
   prompt   Import Text File dialogue box
   respond   *a*) change directory to c:\r13cust
             b) change File Type to Text files
             c) pick **report_1.txt**
             d) pick OK
   prompt   Edit Mtext dialogue box
   with   the text file in the display area
   respond   pick OK.

4 The text file will be imported into the drawing as Fig. 11.7.

5 The drawing can now be saved, but NOT AS COUPLING!

6 This completes the import text exercise and you can now exit AutoCAD.

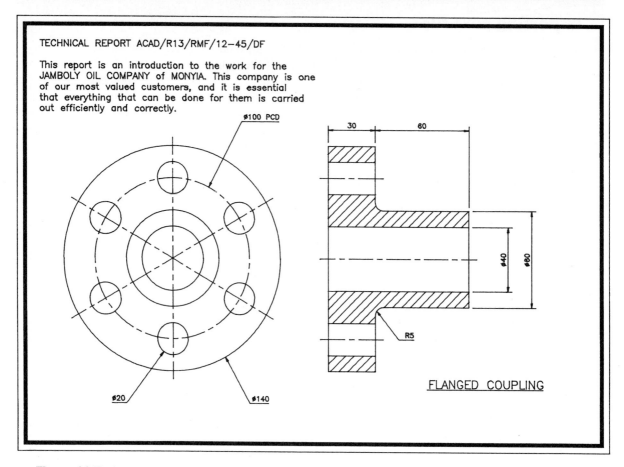

TECHNICAL REPORT ACAD/R13/RMF/12—45/DF

This report is an introduction to the work for the
JAMBOLY OIL COMPANY of MONYIA. This company is one
of our most valued customers, and it is essential
that everything that can be done for them is carried
out efficiently and correctly.

ø100 PCD

30   60

ø40   ø60

R5

FLANGED COUPLING

ø20   ø140

Figure 11.7 Imported a text file into an AutoCAD drawing.

Summary

1 AutoCAD Release 13 supports many different file formats.
2 Most formats can be exported and imported.
3 Export files can be used with many other software packages.
4 Only DXF imported files give a true 'definition' of a drawing as they import layers and all drawing geometry.
5 Import and export commands can be activated:
  a) from the keyboard with ???OUT and ???IN
  b) from the menu bar with File-Import/Export and altering the file type format.
6 Text files can be imported with the MTEXT command.

Activity

I have not included any activity with this chapter as the exercises have been quite involved.

Chapter 12

Object linking and embedding

Working with AutoCAD Release 13 through the Windows environment permits drawing data to be transferred between different Windows application packages and is termed Object Linking and Embedding (**OLE**). OLE is achieved using the Windows **CLIP-BOARD** package which allows the user to:

1 Export drawings from AutoCAD and import them into other application packages.
2 Edit drawings while working in these application packages.
3 Copy drawings into a current drawing.

To demonstrate object linking and embedding, I have decided on a word processor application and will use the **WRITE** windows package as all users should have access to it – it is a standard 'issue' with Windows.

Linking a drawing

To investigating how an AutoCAD drawing is 'linked' to another application software package, we will write a technical report and incorporate our coupling drawing into this report.

1 Start AutoCAD and open C:\R13CUST\COUPLING.

2 With layer 0 current, add a rectangular border 380×270 from the origin point 0,0 – remember we erased this border for the data exchange chapter.

3 Move the complete drawing from 0,0 by @2,2.

4 Now save the drawing twice, with the file names:
   a) C:\R13CUST\COUPLING
   b) C:\R13CUST\CPLNG

   You will appreciate why later in the chapter.

5 From the menu bar select **Edit–Copy View**
   prompt   _copylink
   and   nothing else!

6 Select the left icon in the Title Bar and:
   prompt   pull-down menu
   respond   pick **Switch To...**
   prompt   Task List dialogue box
   respond   **double left-click on Program Manager**
   prompt   Program Manager screen
   respond   *a)* activate **Accessories**
              b) double left-click on Write
   prompt   Write [Untitled] screen
   respond   maximize the screen

7 From the menu bar select **Character**
                                  Fonts...
prompt   Font dialogue box
respond   set the following:
            a) font: **Times New Roman**
            b) size: **10**
            c) pick OK.

8 Enter the following lines of text, remembering <R> at the end of every line:

TECHNICAL REPORT ACAD/R13/RMF/145-98/DG
The couplings are for the JAMBOLY OIL COMPANY of MONYIA
and will be used in their new oil installation in the GONDOVIAN
desert. The weather conditions in this environment are rather harsh, as
the average day temperature is 38 degC and in the evening the
temperature can drop to -50 degC. The prevailing wind is from
the South East and can gust up to 150 km/hr.
These conditions are the main reasons for using the new
material CASPUTIUM in the construction of the coupling.

9 From the menu bar select **Edit**
                                  Paste Link.

10 The coupling drawing will be 'pasted into' the report at the end of the text as Fig. 12.1.
Note: I've re-sized the drawing for effect.

11 From the menu bar select **File**
                                  Save As
prompt   Save As dialogue box
respond   *a*) directory: **c:\r13cust**
            b) file name: **report_2**
            c) pick OK.

12 Select the left icon from the Title bar and:
prompt   pull-down menu
respond   pick **Close**
prompt   Program Manager screen
respond   pick left icon from Title bar
prompt   pull-down menu
respond   pick **Switch To...**
prompt   Task List dialogue box
respond   **double left-click on AutoCAD-[COUPLING.DWG]**

13 You will be returned to your original drawing.

14 *Note*. The process of **SWITCHING** from an AutoCAD drawing to another Windows
package (e.g. Write) is very useful, and you should become proficient with this process.

15 Now exit AutoCAD and pick YES to save changes.

TECHNICAL REPORT ACAD/R13/RMF/145-98/DG

The couplings are for the JAMBOLY OIL COMPANY of MONYIA
and will be used in their new installation in the GONDOVIAN
desert.

The weather conditions in this environment are rather harsh, as
the average day temperature is 38 degC and in the evening the
temperature can drop to -50 degC. The prevailing wind is from
the South East and can gust up to 150 km/hr.

These conditions are the main reasons for using the new
material CASPUTIUM in the construction of the coupling.

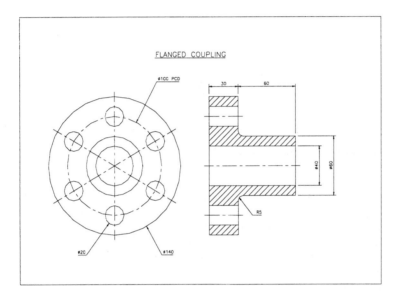

Figure 12.1 Original drawing and report.

Editing a linked drawing

AutoCAD drawings which are linked to other packages can be altered from within:
a) the application package
b) AutoCAD itself.
In this section we will investigate both methods.

Altering from Write

1 Start AutoCAD but *do not* open any drawing.

2 Switch to Program Manager and activate the Write package.

3 Maximize the screen then File–Open and:
a) directory: **c:\r13cust**
b) pick file **report_2.wri**
c) pick OK
   prompt   Write message.
            This document contains links to other documents. Do you want to update
            links now?
   respond **No** (at present).

4 The report document will be displayed with the original coupling drawing.

5 Move the cursor down into the drawing area and:
a) the drawing 'block' turns black
b) double left-click in this block area
c) AutoCAD drawing screen with COUPLING drawing.

6 We will now modify the coupling by altering the right view so:
a) erase the hatching
b) change the six horizontal 'hole lines' to layer HID
c) complete the right view as an 'outside elevation' with:
   i)   a vertical line on layer OUT
   ii) four horizontal lines on layer HID for the holes
   iii) two centre lines on layer CL (you should understand these changes?).

7 Select **File–Save** to update C:\R13CUST\COUPLING.

8 Switch back to the Task List and select Write-REPORT_2.WRI.

9 The drawing in the document will have been modified to include the alterations made
in AutoCAD – Fig. 12.2.

10 Save the report as report_2.

11 Select File–Exit to quit Write and switch back to AutoCAD.

12 Exit AutoCAD.

TECHNICAL REPORT ACAD/R13/RMF/145-98/DG

The couplings are for the JAMBOLY OIL COMPANY of MONYIA
and will be used in their new installation in the GONDOVIAN
desert.
The weather conditions in this environment are rather harsh, as
the average day temperature is 38 degC and in the evening the
temperature can drop to -50 degC. The prevailing wind is from
the South East and can gust up to 150 km/hr.
These conditions are the main reasons for using the new
material CASPUTIUM in the construction of the coupling.

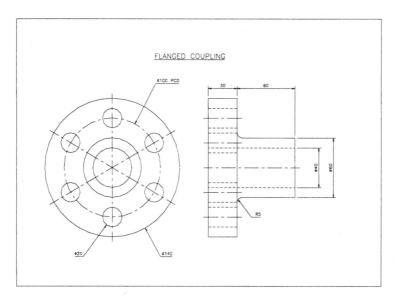

Figure 12.2 Alteration from Write.

Altering from AutoCAD

1 Start AutoCAD and open C:\R13CUST\COUPLING which should be displayed with the previous alterations to the right view.

2 Use the STRETCH (crossing) command and:
 a) stretch the right end (including three dimensions) of the right view by @**18,0**
 b) stretch the left end (including one dimension) of the right view by @**–4,0**.

3 Select **File–Save** to update COUPLING.

4 Switch to the Program Manager and activate Write.

5 Maximize the screen and open document **report_2.wri** from the C:\R13CUST directory and:
 prompt *update links* massage
 respond pick **Yes**.

6 The document will be displayed with the stretched coupling – Fig. 12.3.

7 Save this document as report_2.

8 *a*) Close Write
 b) Switch back to AutoCAD COUPLING
 c) Exit AutoCAD.

TECHNICAL REPORT ACAD/R13/RMF/145-98/DG

The couplings are for the JAMBOLY OIL COMPANY of MONYIA and will be used in their new installation in the GONDOVIAN desert.
The weather conditions in this environment are rather harsh, as the average day temperature is 38 degC and in the evening the temperature can drop to -50 degC. The prevailing wind is from the South East and can gust up to 150 km/hr.
These conditions are the main reasons for using the new material CASPUTIUM in the construction of the coupling.

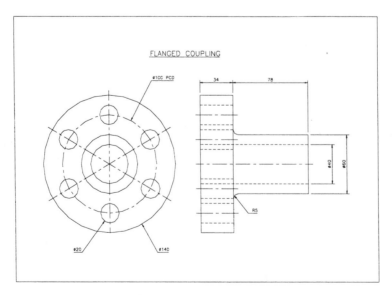

Figure 12.3 Alteration from AutoCAD.

Embedding a drawing

Embedding is a similar process to linking, and we will discuss the differences later in this chapter. To demonstrate the process, we will create a new drawing and embed it into the report document. This is not good practice as the document already contains a linked drawing (the coupling). Drawings should really be either linked or embedded, but we are embedding into the existing report:

a) to show that linking and embedding are permissible in the one report

b) to save the writing of a new report.

1 Start AutoCAD and open your standard sheet.

2 Refer to Fig. 12.4 and draw the component as shown. Use layers correctly and add some other refinements of your choice.

3 Save the drawing as C:\R13CUST\ENDCAP.

4 From the menu bar select **Edit**
> **Copy**

prompt   Select objects

respond   **window the screen then right-click**.

5 Switch to the Program Manager and activate Write.

6 Maximize the screen and open **report_2.wri** from the c:\r13cust directory and:

prompt   Update links message (remember COUPLING is linked to this report)

respond   pick **No**

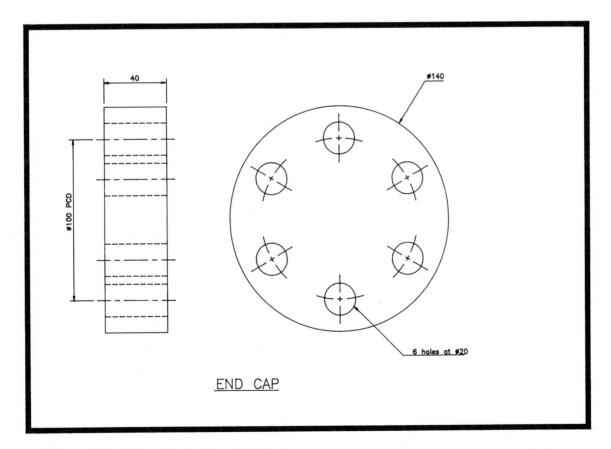

END CAP

Figure 12.4   Endcap drawing for embedding.

7 The document with the stretched coupling will be displayed.

8 Move the cursor below the coupling block.

9 From the menu bar select **Edit–Paste**

10 The end cap drawing will be pasted into the document – Fig. 12.5.

11 Save the document as **report_2.wri** and pick No to the update embedded objects message.

12 Close Write (No to message) and switch back to the AutoCAD end cap drawing.

13 Do not exit AutoCAD.

TECHNICAL REPORT ACAD/R13/RMF/145-98/DG

The couplings are for the JAMBOLY OIL COMPANY of MONYIA and will be used in their new installation in the GONDOVIAN desert.
The weather conditions in this environment are rather harsh, as the average day temperature is 38 degC and in the evening the temperature can drop to -50 degC. The prevailing wind is from the South East and can gust up to 150 km/hr.
These conditions are the main reasons for using the new material CASPUTIUM in the construction of the coupling.

TECHNICAL REPORT ACAD/R13/RMF/145-98/DG

The couplings are for the JAMBOLY OIL COMPANY of MONYIA and will be used in their new installation in the GONDOVIAN desert.
The weather conditions in this environment are rather harsh, as the average day temperature is 38 degC and in the evening the temperature can drop to -50 degC. The prevailing wind is from the South East and can gust up to 150 km/hr.
These conditions are the main reasons for using the new material CASPUTIUM in the construction of the coupling.

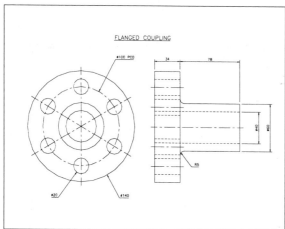

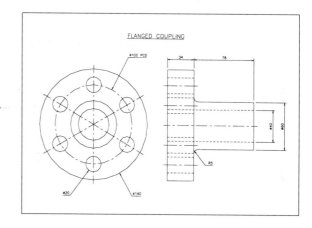

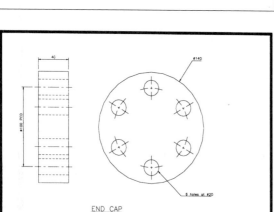

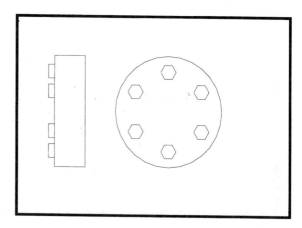

Figure 12.5 Embedded drawing.

Figure 12.6 Editing the embedded drawing.

Editing an embedded drawing

Embedded drawings can *only be edited from within the document in which they are embedded*, so:

1 Begin a new drawing and:
   a) pick **Yes** to save changes
   b) accept the default name.

2 Switch to Program Manager and activate Write.

3 Maximize the screen and open **report_2.wri** and:
   prompt   Update links message
   respond   pick **No**

4 The document with the linked coupling and the embedded end cap will be displayed.

5 Move into the end cap 'block' and:
   prompt   the block turns black
   respond   **double left-click in the block**
   prompt   AutoCAD with end cap drawing.

6 Modify the drawing by:
   a) erase all dimensions and text
   b) add six hexagons, centred on the small circle centre, inscribed in a circle of radius 10
   c) erase the six small circles and their centre lines
   d) erase the centre lines and hidden lines in the left view
   e) complete the left view by adding 'bolt heads' of height 8 to left vertical line of the left view, using the six hexagons from the right view.

7 From the menu bar select **File** and:
   prompt   pull-down menu
   with   a new item
               Update REPORT_2.WRI
               (this item is **ALWAYS** added to the file options with an embedded drawing)
   respond   **pick this new item**.

8 Switch back to Write-REPORT_2.WRI and the embedded end cap drawing should be displayed with the current modifications – Fig. 12.6.

9 Save this report – name?

10 *Task*.
   Exit Write and AutoCAD and think about the messages!

Linking vs embedding

Linking and embedding are very similar processes. The correct terminology is Object Linking and Embedding (**OLE**) and is a Windows facility. Both options allow an AutoCAD drawing to be 'imported' into Windows application software, but they differ in the manner in which the drawing data is stored.

a) *Linking*: this actually makes a link between the original (**source**) drawing and the destination (**client**) document. The link informs the destination document of where the source drawing data can be found. The linked drawing can be edited from the document or from AutoCAD, both methods updating the source drawing and the destination document. Linking should be used if the document has to have automatic updates when the source drawing is altered. Only complete named drawings can be linked.

b) *Embedding:* an embedded drawing is actually copied into the destination document and is then not directly associated with the source drawing. An embedded drawing can only be edited from the actual document and the original source drawing is untouched.

Embedding should be used when the source drawing is to stay unaltered and the drawing in the document is to be altered. It is possible to select individual objects (e.g. window) for embedding.

Copying drawings

AutoCAD entities can be copied into CLIPBOARD for insertion into other software or for insertion into another AutoCAD drawing, which is the exercise we will now investigate.

1 Start AutoCAD and open the **CPLNG** drawing from the C:\R13CUST directory. You should realise why the coupling drawing was saved with another name. What would be displayed if we had opened the COUPLING drawing?

2 Erase all dimensions from the drawing.

3 From the Standard toolbar select the Copy icon and:

prompt   _copyclip
then   Select objects
respond window the complete drawing then right-click.

4 Switch to Program Manager and activate Clipboard Viewer from the Main windows directory.
Question: is coupling drawing there?

5 a) Close Clipboard
b) Switch back to AutoCAD-[CPLNG.DWG].

6 Open the ENDCAP drawing previously saved and pick No to any save changes message. The end cap drawing should be displayed as originally drawn and has not been affected by the modifications which were made for the embedding exercise.

7 Erase all dimensions from the drawing and move the complete component as far to the right as possible.

8 From the Standard toolbar select the Paste icon and:
> *prompt*   `_pasteclip`
> *then*   `Insertion point` and enter **20,20**
> *prompt*   `X scale...` and enter **0.35**
> *prompt*   `Y scale...` and enter **0.85**
> *prompt*   `Rotation...` and enter **0**.

9 The cplng drawing will be inserted from Clipboard into the current drawing – Fig. 12.7.

10 This completes the exercise, so exit AutoCAD and have a rest!

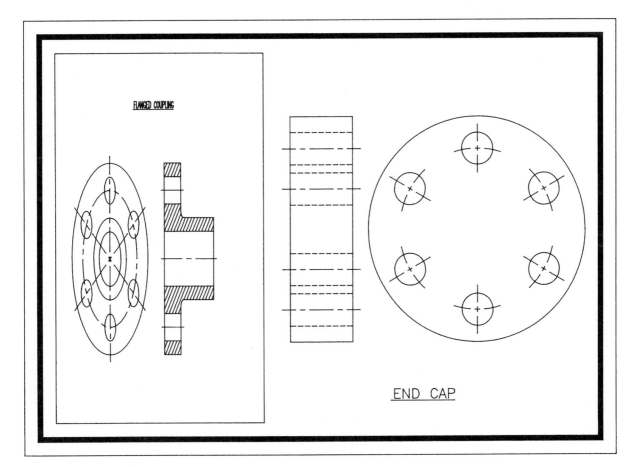

Figure 12.7   Copied drawing pasted into an existing drawing.

General note

The exercises in this chapter have introduced OLE to the reader. The concept is very powerful and there are more options than have been demonstrated. You should have the ability (and confidence) to try these other options.

Summary

1 AutoCAD drawings can be 'linked' or 'embedded' to other Windows application packages.
2 AutoCAD drawings can be copied into other AutoCAD drawings.
3 The Windows package CLIPBOARD is used as the 'transfer' medium.
4 The differences between linking and embedding are:

Linking	*Embedding*
complete drawings	any selected entities
edited from AutoCAD	edited from document only
edited from document	source drawing unaltered
source drawing altered.	

Activity

No activity has been included for this chapter.

Chapter 13

AutoLISP

AutoLISP is a programming language which has been developed for use with AutoCAD. It allows the user to customize routines that can increase drawing productivity and has many uses including:
a) parametric drawing
b) drawing 'interrogation'.

It is not my intention to teach AutoLISP in this chapter, but I will introduce AutoLISP's capabilities and let the reader decide if they want to proceed any further with the topic.

Because it is a programming language, AutoLISP has a command structure and syntax of its own. AutoLISP 'commands' can be contained within a program, or entered directly from the keyboard. All AutoLISP programmed routines are text files, written by the user with the extension **.LSP**.

What can AutoLISP do?

As an introduction to AutoLISP, we will write a simple routine and 'run it'. You should realize that the 'program' may mean nothing to you at this stage.

1 Open your STDA3 standard sheet.

2 At the command line enter **SHELL** <R> and:
prompt   OS Command
enter   **EDIT C:\R13CUST\TEST.LSP**
prompt   MS DOS text editor
respond   enter the following lines of text, remembering <R> at the end of each line:

```
(defun C:TEST ()
   (setq C (list 100 100))
   (setq R 10)
   (repeat 5
       (command "CIRCLE" C R)
       (setq R (+ R 10))
   )
   (setq CEN (list 250 100))
   (setq RAD 10)
   (setq SIDE 4)
   (repeat 6
       (command "POLYGON" SIDE CEN "C" RAD)
       (setq RAD (+ RAD 10))
       (setq SIDE (+ SIDE 1))
   )
   (setq P1 (list 100 200))
   (setq P2 (list 200 15))
   (command "TEXT" P1 "12" "0" "AutoCAD")
   (command "COLOUR" "GREEN")
   (command "TEXT" P2 "10" "5" "AutoLISP")
)
```

3 From the menu bar select File–Save As and check:

   a) directory: **c:\r13cust**
   b) file name: **TEST.LSP**
   c) pick OK.

4 Select File–Exit to return to AutoCAD.

5 At the command line enter **(load "TEST")** and if there are no errors in the routine:

   prompt   C:TEST
   enter   **TEST** <R>

6 The drawing screen should display:

   a) five concentric circles
   b) six 'concentric' polygons of increasing size
   c) two text items – one red and one green.

7 *Note.*

   a) at this stage we will not discuss this routine
   b) what is the colour displayed in the Object Properties dialogue box? Can you change it back to the current layer colour?

8 The routines that follow have to be entered using a text editor and there is no shortcut. When the routine has been entered and 'run', we will then discuss the new concepts introduced.

Variables and commands

AutoLISP works with variable names and all AutoCAD commands can be included in AutoLISP routines.

Routine A1

1 Still have the result of the TEST routine on the screen?

2 At the command line enter **SHELL** <R> and:

   prompt   OS Command
   enter   **EDIT C:\R13CUST\PROGA_1.LSP** <R>
   prompt   MS DOS text editor
   respond enter the following lines of text:

```
(defun C:proga_1 ()                          – line 1
   (setq a 200 b 190 c 345 d 245)            – line 2
   (setq pt1 (list a b))                     – line 3
   (setq pt2 (list c d))                     – line 4
   (command "LINE" pt1 pt2 "")               – line 5
)                                            – line 6
```

3 File–Save As with directory c:\r13cust and file name PROGA_1.LSP then File–Exit.

4 At the command line enter **(load "proga_1")** <R> and: – line 7

   prompt   C:PROGA_1   – line 8
   enter   **PROGA_1** <R>   – line 9.

5 A line will be drawn in the top right area of the screen.

6 *Explanation*

line 1:   the routine name line and (at this stage) it is recommended that all AutoLISP routines start with this format.

           (:   all routines start with (
           defun: define function
           C:xxx: routine name
           ( ):   define variables used

line 2:   set four variables, i.e. a with 200, b with 190, etc. This is equivalent to LET A=200 in other programming languages. The setq is **SET QUOTE** and is used to set all variables

line 3:   setting a *coordinate pair* using the **LIST** function. The point pt1 is set to the values of a and b, i.e. pt1 (200,190). Note the use of the brackets. There is the same number of opening **(** brackets as closing **)** brackets in a line

line 4:   set pt2 as (345,245)

line 5:   activate the AutoCAD command LINE, and draw a line from pt1 to pt2. The " " after pt2 is equivalent to a <RETURN> key press. Note that the AutoCAD command is within " ", i.e. "LINE"

line 6:   the closing **)** for the routine, to 'match' the opening **(** in line 1

line 7:   all AutoLISP routines must be loaded before they can be used and the format is **(load "progname")**

line 8:   if the routine does not have any errors, the prompt line will always display **C:progname**

line 9:   entering **progname** will 'run' the routine after it has been loaded.

Routine A2

1 At the command line enter **SHELL** <R> then:
EDIT C:\R13CUST\PROGA_2.LSP <R> and:
prompt   text editor
respond enter the following program:

```
(defun C:proga_2 ()
(setq x1 30)
(setq y1 (* x1 8))                              – line 1
(setq WID (/ x1 5))                             – line 2
(setq P1 (list x1 y1))                          – line 3
(command "PLINE" P1 "W" WID "0" "@100<–77" "")  – line 4
)                                               – line 5.
```

2 File–Save As then File–Exit to return to drawing screen.

3 At command line enter **(load "proga_2")** and:
prompt   C:PROGA_2
enter   **PROGA_2** <R>.

4 An inclined polyline of varying width will be displayed.

5 *Explanation.*

line 1: set a variable y1 with the value of x1*8. The (* x1 8) is the manner in which arithmetic operations are achieved with AutoLISP and is called **Reverse Polish Notation**.

line 2: set a variable WID with the value of x1/5.

line 3: set a point P1 having the co-ordinates (x1,y1)

line 4: activate the AutoCAD PLINE command with:

   a) the start point at P1

   b) the width option activated with "W"

   c) a start width of WID

   d) a zero end width entered as "0"

   e) the endpoint of the polyline segment relative to P1 entered as "@100<−77"

   f) end the polyline command with " "

line 5: the closing) to match the opening (.

Routine A3

1 Using SHELL with EDIT C:\R13CUST\PROGA_3.LSP, enter the following routine:

```
(defun C:PROGA_3 ()
    (setq a 200 b 240 R 20)          – line 1
    (setq C1 (list a b))             – line 2
    (setq C2 (list b a))             – line 3
    (setq R1 (+ R 8))                – line 4
    (setq R2 (– R 8))                – line 5
    (command "CIRCLE" C1 R1)         – line 6
    (command "CIRCLE" C2 R2)
    (setq TX "AutoLISP Routines")    – line 7
    (setq TPT (list R R))            – line 8
    (command "TEXT" TPT R2 R1 TX)    – line 9.
)
```

2 File–Save As then File–Exit.

3 *a*) Load the routine with (load "proga_3")

   b) Run the routine with proga_3.

4 Screen will display two circles and an item of text.

5 At this stage your screen should resemble Fig. 13.1 and the drawing can now be saved.

6 *Explanation.*

line 1: set three variables, i.e. a=200, b=240, R=20

line 2: set the point C1 with coordinates a,b, i.e. (200,240)

line 3: set point C2 to (b,a)

line 4: set the variable R1 with the value R+8

line 5: set R2 to R−8

line 6: activate the CIRCLE command with:

   a) centre point at C1, i.e. 200,240

   b) radius R1, i.e. 28

line 7: set the variable TX with the text item 'AutoLISP Routines' which is within " " quotes

line 8: set the point TPT with coordinates (R,R)

line 9: activate the TEXT command with:

   a) start point at point TPT which is (?,?)

   b) a height of R2

   c) a rotation angle of R1

   d) TX as the item of text.

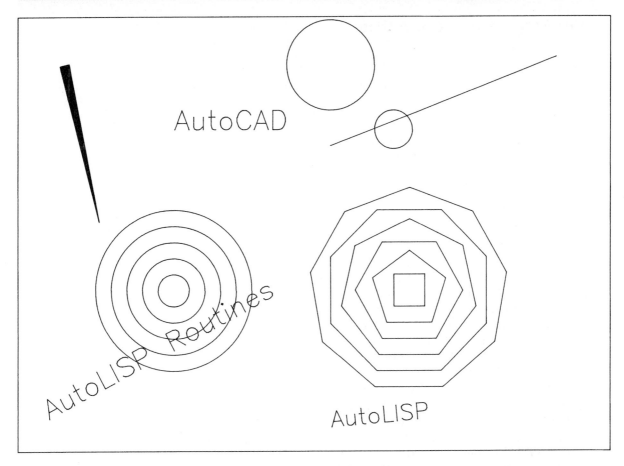

Figure 13.1 AutoLISP routines PROGA_1, PROGA_2 and PROG_3.

Task

Before leaving these exercises enter at the command line:

a) **!a**   prompt 200 (where **! is shift 1**)
b) **!pt1**   prompt (200 190)
c) **!y1**   prompt 240
d) **!WID**   prompt 6
e) **!P1**   prompt (100 200)
f) **!C2**   prompt (240 200)
g) **!TX**   prompt "AutoLISP Routines"
h) **!TPT**   prompt (20 20)
i) **!X**   nil

The key *!* (**PLING**) will display the contents of the variable stores used in AutoLISP routines, i.e. store 'a' contains the number 200; store pt1 contains the *coordinate pair* (200,190), etc.

Working with coordinates

Coordinates can be used with AutoLISP routines:

a) by entering the coordinates within " ", e.g. "200,100"; "35,267"

b) using the AutoLISP function **LIST**, e.g. (setq P1 (list 150 120)) will set P1 to (150,120).

There are two other AutoLISP functions which can be used with coordinates, these being **car** and **cadr** where:

a) car: returns the *x* coordinate of a point

b) cadr: returns the *y* coordinate of a point.

Routine B1

The program which follows is quite long but includes four routines, so:

1 Open your standard sheet.

2 At the command line enter **SHELL** <R> then:
EDIT C:\R13CUST\PROGB_1.LSP <R>

```
(defun C:PROGB_1 ()
    (setq PT1 (list 50 100))                        – line 1
    (setq PT2 (list 200 80))
    (setq A (car PT1) B (cadr PT2))
    (setq PT3 (list A B))
    (setq PT4 (list (car PT2) (cadr PT1)))
    (command "LINE" PT1 PT4 PT2 PT3 "C")
    (setq X (+ (car PT1) (cadr PT2)))               – line 2
    (setq Y (– (car PT2) (car PT1)))
    (setq RAD (/ (car PT2) 5))
    (command "CIRCLE" (list X Y) RAD)
    (setq W (list 280 70))                          – line 3
    (setq ID (/ (cadr W) 5))
    (setq OD (* (/ (car W) (cadr W)) 4))
    (command "DONUT" ID OD W "")
    (setq K1 (list 190 120))                        – line 4
    (setq HT (/ (car K1) 20))
    (setq ROT (/ (cadr K1) 10))
    (setq WORD "CAR_and_CADR")
    (command "TEXT" K1 HT ROT WORD)
)
```

3 File–Save As then File–Exit.

4 Load and run the program with:

a) **(load "PROGB_1")** <R>

b) **PROGB_1** <R>.

5 The screen will display:

a) a rectangle

b) a circle

c) a donut

d) an item of text.

6 *Explanation.*

line 1: a routine to draw a rectangle. The variables PT1 and PT2 are set using the LIST function. PT3 is set from variables A (x coord of PT1) and B (y coord of PT2). PT4 is set with the LIST function using the x coord of PT2 and y coord of PT1

line 2: a circle routine. The circle centre is (*X,Y*) and radius RAD where:

    X: (x coord of PT1)+(y coord of PT2)

    Y: (x coord of PT2)−(x coord of PT1)

    RAD: (x coord of PT2)/5.

line 3: a donut routine

    The donut centre is W (280,70) and:

    ID: (y coord of W)/5

    OD: [(x coord of W)/(y coord of W)]*4.

line 4: a text routine

    K1:   the text start point

    HT: the height is (x coord K1)/20

    ROT: the rotation angle (y coord of K1)/10

    WORD: the text item.

7 The following list gives the contents of several of the variables used in the program.

Variable	Value
PT1	(50 100)
X	130
Y	150
RAD	40
W	(280 70)
ID	14
HT	9

a) Are these the same as your variables?

b) Can you work out how these figures were obtained?

8 Do not exit this drawing, but proceed to the next exercise.

The GET functions

The previous routines have all had variable values set within the programs. It is possible to set variables by keyboard entry and by selecting points on the screen while a program is being 'run'. This is achieved with the AutoLISP **GET** functions.

1 Still have the result of PROGB_1 on the screen?

2 Enter the following program:
SHELL–EDIT C:\R13CUST\PROGC_1.LSP
(defun C:PROGC_1 ()
    (setq WID1 (getint "Enter start width :"))   – line 1
    (setq WID2 (getint "Enter end width :"))
    (setq P1 (getpoint "Pick a start point "))   – line 2
    (setq P3 (getpoint "Pick an opposite diagonal "))
    (setq P2 (list (car P1) (cadr P3)))   – line 3
    (setq P4 (list (car P3) (cadr P1)))
    (command "PLINE" P1 "W" WID1 WID2 P2 P3 P4 "C")   – line 4.
)

3 File–Save As then File–Exit.

4 Load the program with **(load "PROGC_1")** and:
prompt   C:PROCG_1
enter   **PROGC_1 <R>**
prompt   Enter start width :
enter   **20 <R>**
prompt   Enter end width :
enter   **20 <R>**
prompt   Pick a start point
respond   **pick any point towards lower left of screen**
prompt   Pick an opposite diagonal
respond   **pick any point towards upper right of screen.**

5 A closed polyline rectangle of width 20 will be displayed.

6 Enter **PROGC_1** again and:
a) start width: enter **5**
b) end width: enter **0**
c) points: pick within rectangle.

7 At this stage your drawing should resemble Fig. 13.2 and can now be saved.

8 *Explanation.*
   line 1:   set a variable (WID1) using the GETINT function. The getint function allows any numeric value to be entered from the keyboard when an AutoLISP program is run. If text is added within " ", then this text will be displayed at the command line.
               Thus 'Enter start width' will be displayed, and as 20 was entered from the keyboard, the variable WID1 is set to 20.
   line 2:   set a point (P1) using the GETPOINT function. The getpoint function allows a coordinate to be entered:
               a) from the keyboard
               b) by picking a point on the screen.
               Thus 'Pick a point' will be displayed, and when any point on the screen is 'picked', variable P1 is set with the co-ordinates of this picked point.
   line 3:   using the picked point P1 and P3 to set another point.
   line 4:   the polyline command using the variable inputs.

9 The GET functions include:

   a) getpoint: user input as a point
   b) getreal: user input as a real number
   c) getstring: user input as a string
   d) getint: user input as an integer
   e) getvar: user access to system variables.

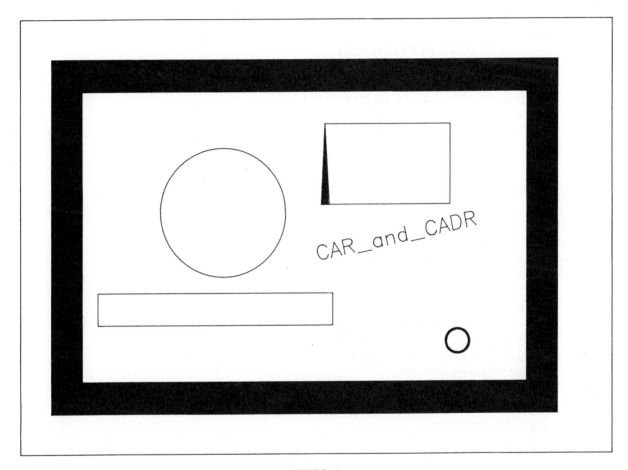

Figure 13.2   AutoLISP routines PROGB_1 and PROGC_1.

Repeated operations

AutoLISP routines are particularly suited to repeated operations and will be demonstrated with several routines.

1 Open your standard sheet.

2 **SHELL-EDIT C:\R13CUST\PROGD_1.LSP** then enter:
```
(defun C:PROGD_1 ()
    (setq a 20 b 20 c 180 d 240)
    (repeat 14                                              – line 1
        (setq P1 (list a b) P3 (list c d))
        (setq P2 (list (car P3) (cadr P1)))
        (setq P4 (list (car P1) (cadr P3)))
        (command "LINE" P1 P2 P3 P4 "C")
        (setq a (+ a 5) b (+ b 5))
        (setq c (– c 5) d (– d 5))
    )                                                       – line 2
)                                                           – line 3.
```

3 File–Save As then File–Exit.

4 Write another routine with:
  a) **SHELL-EDIT C:\R13CUST\PROGD_2.LSP**
  b) the following lines:
```
(defun C:PROGD_2 ()
        (setq p 210 q 15 r 350 s 15)
        (setq w1 12 w2 0)
        (repeat 10                                          – line 4
          (setq PT1 (list p q) PT2 (list r s))
          (command "PLINE" PT1 "W" w1 w2 PT2 "")
          (setq q (+ q 15) s (+ s 25))
          (setq w1 (– w1 1))
        )                                                   – line 5
)                                                           – line 6.
```

5 File–Save As then File–Exit.

6 From the menu bar select **Tools**
                    Applications...

prompt   Load AutoLISP,ADS and ARX Files dialogue box
respond   pick **File...**
prompt   Select AutoLISP,ADS and ARX Files dialogue box
respond   *a*) directory: **c:\r13cust**
         b) files: ***.lsp**
         c) pick **progd_1.lsp**
         d) pick OK
prompt   Load AutoLISP..... dialogue box
with   C:\R13CUST\PROGD_1.LSP listed
respond   pick **Load**
prompt   Loading C:\R13CUST\PROGD_1.LSP

7 Run the routine by entering **PROGD_1** <R>.

8 Load routine PROGD_2.LSP using the Tools–Applications selection and run the program.

9 The result of these two routines is Fig. 13.3.

Figure 13.3 AutoLISP routines PROGD_1 and PROGD_2.

10 *Explanation.*

line 1: the start of the repeat loop

line 2: the end of the repeat loop. All functions and commands within the loop brackets will be repeated 14 times. We are drawing a rectangle then increasing/decreasing the coordinates of the vertices. The LINE command is being activated at each pass of the loop

line 3: the end of the program bracket

line 4: start of repeat loop

line 5: end of repeat loop. A varying width polyline is drawn and the loop alters the start and end points as well as the starting width. The end width is 0 at all times

line 6: end of program bracket.

11 *Task*.

Enter, load and run the following routine which should display Fig. 13.4. There are five different repeat loops within the one routine. Try and reason the various entries in the routine.

```
SHELL-EDIT C:\R13CUST\PROGD_3.LSP
(defun C:PROGD_3 ()
  (setq p 30 q 60 r 5)
  (repeat 10                                     ; start of loop 1
    (setq P1 (list p q))
    (command "CIRCLE" P1 r)
    (setq r (+ r 5) p (+ p 5))
  )                                              ; end of loop 1
  (setq a 70 b 130 ht 3 rot 0 W$ "CAD")
  (repeat 8                                      ; start of loop 2
    (setq S (list a b))
    (command "TEXT" S ht rot W$)
    (setq b (+ b (* ht 2)) ht (+ ht 1) rot (+ rot 10))
  )                                              ; end of loop 2
  (setq k1 160 k2 250)
  (repeat 10                                     ; start of loop 3
    (setq pt1 (list k1 k2))
    (command "LINE" pt1 "@0,10" "@-50,0" "@0,-50" "@10,0" "")
    (setq k1 (+ k1 10) k2 (- k2 10))
  )                                              ; end of loop 3
  (command "LINE" "210,110" "260,110" "260,160" "210,160" "")
  (setq a1 160 a2 50 a3 180 a4 20 a5 80)
  (repeat 9                                      ; start of loop 4
    (setq X1 (list a1 a2) X2 (list a3 a4))
    (setq X3 (list a3 a5) X4 (list a3 a2))
    (command "ARC" "C" X1 X2 X3)
    (command "ARC" "C" X4 X2 X3)
    (setq a1 (+ a1 20) a3 (+ a3 20))
  )                                              ; end of loop 4
  (setq Z1 340 Z2 240 Z3 370 H1 4)
  (repeat 4                                      ; start of loop 5
    (setq PO1 (list Z1 Z2) PO2 (list Z3 Z2))
    (command "TEXT" "F" PO1 PO2 H1 "LISP")
    (setq Z1 (- Z1 20) Z2 (- Z2 15) H1 (+ H1 4))
  )                                              ; end of loop 5
)                                                ; end of program.
```

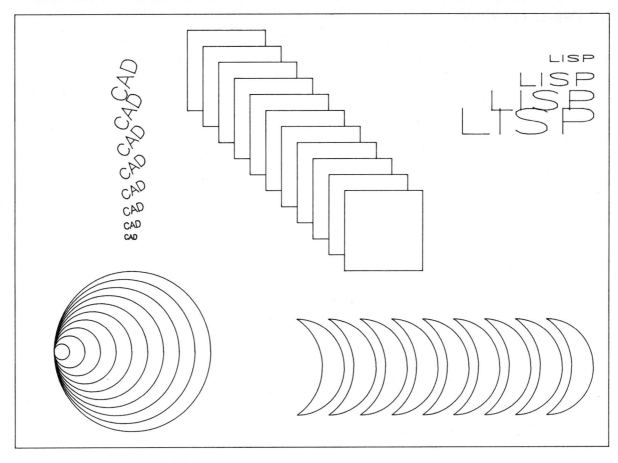

Figure 13.4   AutoLISP routine PROGD_3.LSP.

Other routines

To end this chapter there are two other routines. The first uses the WHILE function for repeated operations and includes 'conditions' in the routine. The second routine is a digital clock 'effect'.

1 Open your standard sheet.

2 SHELL-EDIT C:\R13CUST\PROGE_1.LSP

```
(defun C:PROGE_1 ()
   (setq a 50 b 50 rad 10 c 1)
   (while (< c 20)                              – start of loop
      (setq CT (list a b))
      (command "CIRCLE" CT rad)
      (command "DONUT" "0" "3" CT "")
      (setq a (+ a 10) b (+ b 10) rad (+ rad 10))
      (setq c (1+ c))
      (if (>= a 150)                            – condition loop
          (setq b (– b 15) rad (– rad 15))
      )                                         – end condition
   )                                            – end while
   (setq W "AutoLISP" x 10 y 10 h 5)
   (while (<= x 340)                            – start loop
      (setq P1 (list x y))
      (setq P2 (list (+ x 30) y))
      (command "TEXT" "F" P1 P2 h W)
      (setq P1 P2)
      (setq x (+ x 30) h (+ h 2))
   )                                            – end loop
)                                               – end program
```

3 File–Save As then File–Exit.

4 Load and run PROGE_1 to give the screen effect as Fig. 13.5.

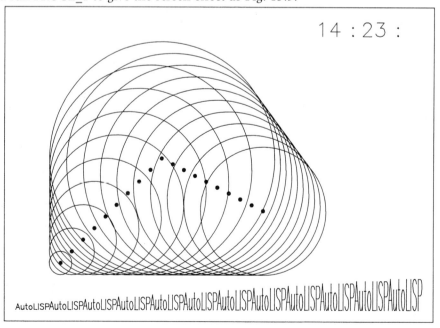

Figure 13.5 AutoLISP routines PROGE_1 and CLOCK.LSP.

5 **SHELL-EDIT C:\R13CUST\CLOCK.LSP** with:

```
(defun C:CLOCK ()
   (textscr)
   (setq h (getint "Enter the hours: "))(terpri)
   (setq m (getint "Enter the minutes: "))(terpri)
   (graphscr)
   (command "TEXT" "275,245" "12" "0" h)
   (command "TEXT" "305,245" "12" "0" ":")
   (command "TEXT" "345,245" "12" "0" ":")
   (repeat 59                                              – minutes loop
      (command "TEXT" "315,245" "12" "0" m)
      (setq s 0 ct 0)
      (repeat 59                                           – seconds loop
         (command "TEXT" "355,245" "12" "0" s)
         (repeat 50 (setq ct (+ ct 1)))
         (command "ERASE" "L" "")
         (setq s (+ s 1))
         (if (= s 59)
            (setq s 0))
      )                                                    – end seconds loop
      (setq m (+ m 1))
      (if (= m 59)
      (setq m 0))
      (command "ERASE" "C" "315,235" "335,265" "")
   )                                                       – end minutes loop
)                                                          – end program.
```

6 Load and run the clock routine which will display a digital clock effect (of sorts) in the top right of the screen. Note that I have not programmed the hours to change.

7 Save your work then exit AutoCAD.

8 This completes the chapter on AutoLISP.

Summary

1 AutoLISP is a programming language written for use with AutoCAD.

2 The functions available with AutoLISP allow all the AutoCAD commands to be programmed.

3 Routines can be written with repeat loops and condition statements can be added.

4 AutoLISP allows drawings to be interrogated.

5 This chapter has been an introduction to the topic. Readers who are interested in AutoLISP are advised to pursue the subject as it is a very powerful productivity tool.

Tutorial 1(a): Lorry icon sizes and attribute information.

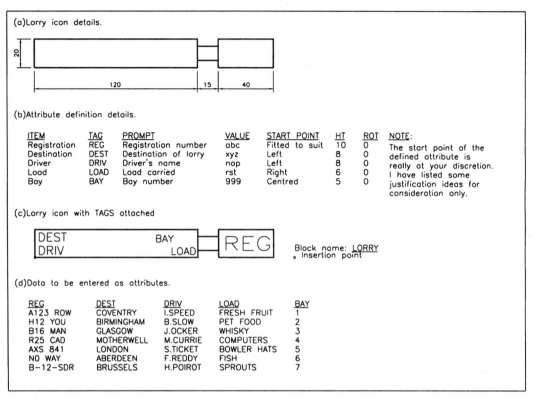

(a)Lorry icon details.

(b)Attribute definition details.

ITEM	TAG	PROMPT	VALUE	START POINT	HT	ROT	NOTE:
Registration	REG	Registration number	abc	Fitted to suit	10	0	
Destination	DEST	Destination of lorry	xyz	Left	8	0	
Driver	DRIV	Driver's name	nop	Left	8	0	
Load	LOAD	Load carried	rst	Right	6	0	
Bay	BAY	Bay number	999	Centred	5	0	

NOTE:
The start point of the defined attribute is really at your discretion. I have listed some justification ideas for consideration only.

(c)Lorry icon with TAGS attached

Block name: LORRY
Insertion point

(d)Data to be entered as attributes.

REG	DEST	DRIV	LOAD	BAY
A123 ROW	COVENTRY	I.SPEED	FRESH FRUIT	1
H12 YOU	BIRMINGHAM	B.SLOW	PET FOOD	2
B16 MAN	GLASGOW	J.OCKER	WHISKY	3
R25 CAD	MOTHERWELL	M.CURRIE	COMPUTERS	4
AXS 841	LONDON	S.TICKET	BOWLER HATS	5
NO WAY	ABERDEEN	F.REDDY	FISH	6
B-12-SDR	BRUSSELS	H.POIROT	SPROUTS	7

Tutorial 1(b): Warehouse loading bay area with attribute details added.

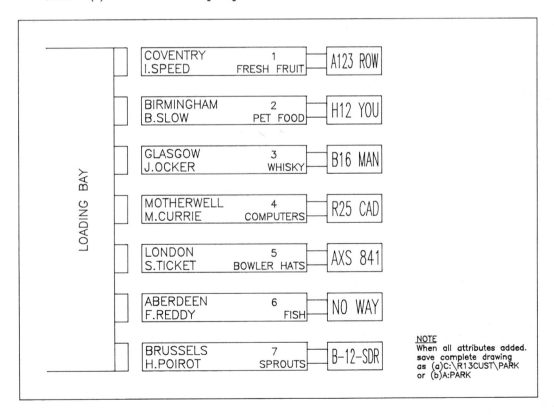

NOTE
When all attributes added. save complete drawing as (a)C:\R13CUST\PARK or (b)A:PARK

Tutorial 2: Warehouse loading bay after attribute editing.

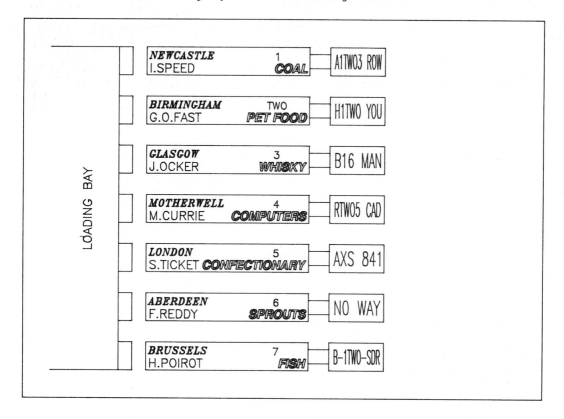

Tutorial 3: Attribute extract files for warehouse loading bay.

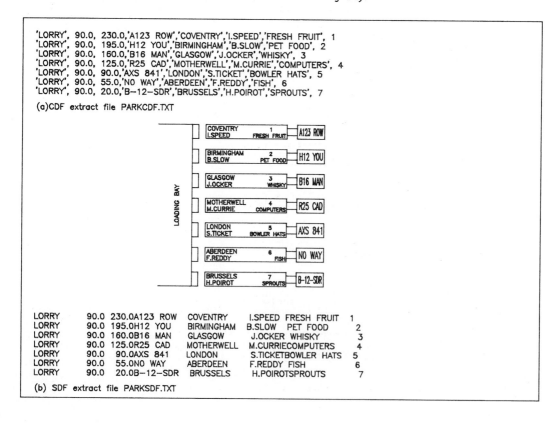

```
'LORRY', 90.0, 230.0,'A123 ROW','COVENTRY','I.SPEED','FRESH FRUIT', 1
'LORRY', 90.0, 195.0,'H12 YOU','BIRMINGHAM','B.SLOW','PET FOOD', 2
'LORRY', 90.0, 160.0,'B16 MAN', 'GLASGOW','J.OCKER','WHISKY', 3
'LORRY', 90.0, 125.0,'R25 CAD','MOTHERWELL','M.CURRIE','COMPUTERS', 4
'LORRY', 90.0, 90.0,'AXS 841','LONDON','S.TICKET','BOWLER HATS', 5
'LORRY', 90.0, 55.0,'NO WAY','ABERDEEN','F.REDDY','FISH', 6
'LORRY', 90.0, 20.0,'B−12−SDR','BRUSSELS','H.POIROT','SPROUTS', 7
```

(a)CDF extract file PARKCDF.TXT

```
LORRY      90.0 230.0A123 ROW    COVENTRY       I.SPEED FRESH FRUIT   1
LORRY      90.0 195.0H12 YOU     BIRMINGHAM     B.SLOW  PET FOOD      2
LORRY      90.0 160.0B16 MAN     GLASGOW        J.OCKER WHISKY        3
LORRY      90.0 125.0R25 CAD     MOTHERWELL     M.CURRIECOMPUTERS     4
LORRY      90.0  90.0AXS 841     LONDON         S.TICKETBOWLER HATS   5
LORRY      90.0  55.0NO WAY      ABERDEEN       F.REDDY FISH          6
LORRY      90.0  20.0B−12−SDR    BRUSSELS       H.POIROTSPROUTS       7
```

(b) SDF extract file PARKSDF.TXT

Tutorial 4(a) Two new linetype definitions for completion of the STADIUM layout
with (a) the linetype sizes given as drawing units (b) the partially
completed linetype descriptors.

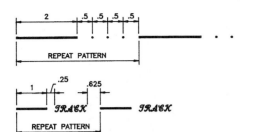

*SECTOR, sector linetype
A,...........................

*TRACK, track linetype
A,........................

*BOUNDARY, boundary linetype
A,1,−.25,["BOUND",ST2,S=.1,R=0,X=−0.1,Y=−0.05],−.625

(a) Linetype definitions   (b) Partial linetype descriptors

NOTE
1. All sizes are given as drawing units.
2. Write the new linetypes in C:\R13CUST\MYLINE.LIN
3. The descriptor for complex linetype BOUNDARY
   is given for reference.
4. Proceed to tutorial 4(b) when the new
   linetypes have been created.

Tutorial 4(b): STADIUM created from customised linetypes.

NOTE
1. Layout at your discretion.
2. Optimise the ltScale value
   to suit.

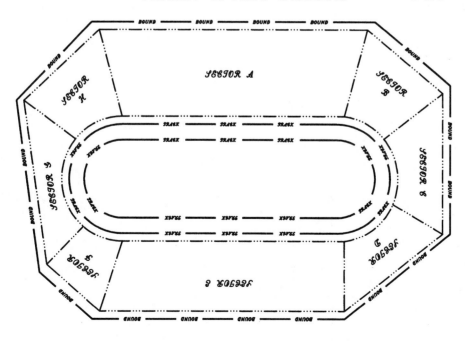

FARMAC SPORTS STADIUM

Tutorial 5: STADIUM drawing with 4 customised hatch patterns added.

FARMAC SPORTS STADIUM

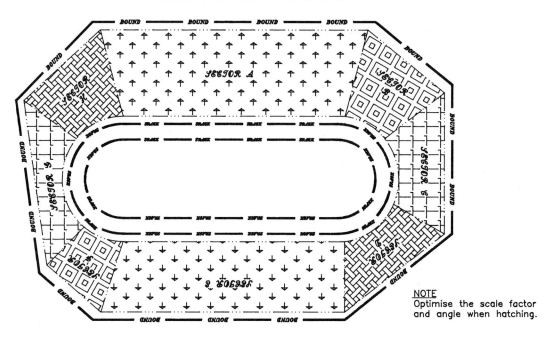

NOTE
Optimise the scale factor
and angle when hatching.

Tutorial 6: Using the information given, create a new hatch pattern ARRHD.PAT.

line 1: origin 0,0; angle 60°
line 2: origin 2.5,0; angle 90°
line 3: origin 5,0; angle 120°

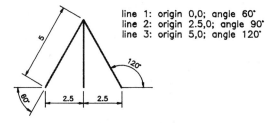

(a)Basic element sizes.

line 1
X1: 5
Y1: 8.66

line 2
X2: 8.66
Y2: 5

line 3
X3: 5
Y3: 8.66

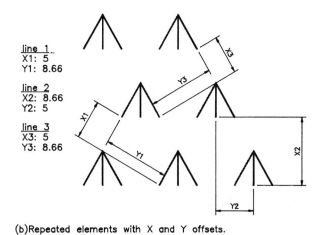

(b)Repeated elements with X and Y offsets.

(c)Using the ARRHD hatch pattern.

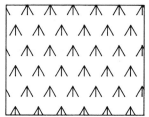

Scale: 1.5
Angle: 0

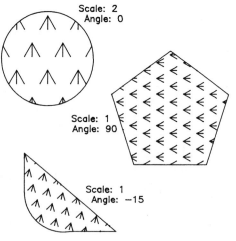

Scale: 2
Angle: 0

Scale: 1
Angle: 90

Scale: 1
Angle: −15

Tutorial 7: Shape activity.
Create the 5 given shapes in a new file called COMP.SHP. Add the compiled shapes to a TV monitor.

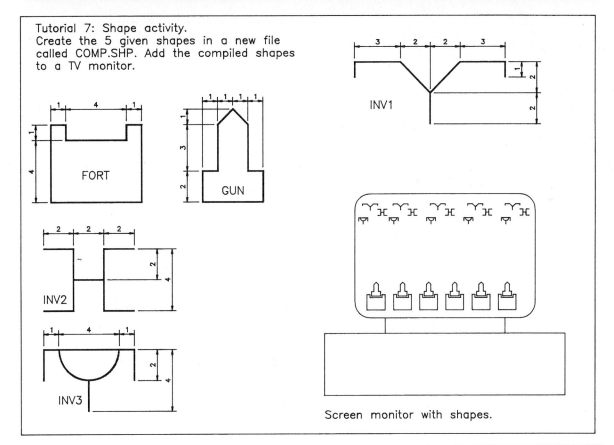

Screen monitor with shapes.

Tutorial 8(a): Block sizes for screen menu SCMEN.MNU

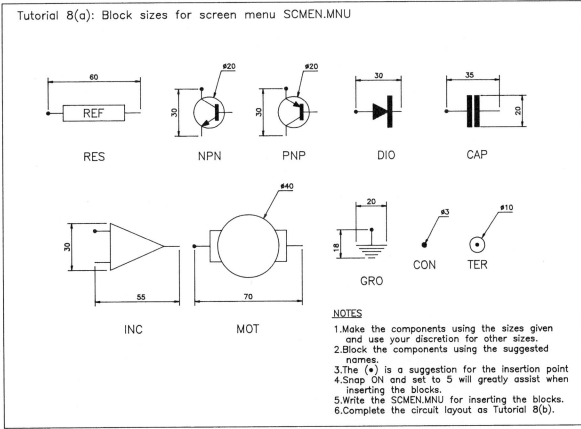

NOTES
1. Make the components using the sizes given and use your discretion for other sizes.
2. Block the components using the suggested names.
3. The (•) is a suggestion for the insertion point
4. Snap ON and set to 5 will greatly assist when inserting the blocks.
5. Write the SCMEN.MNU for inserting the blocks.
6. Complete the circuit layout as Tutorial 8(b).

Tutorial 8(b): Electrical circuit drawn using the blocks from tutorial 8(a)
and the screen menu SCMEN.MNU

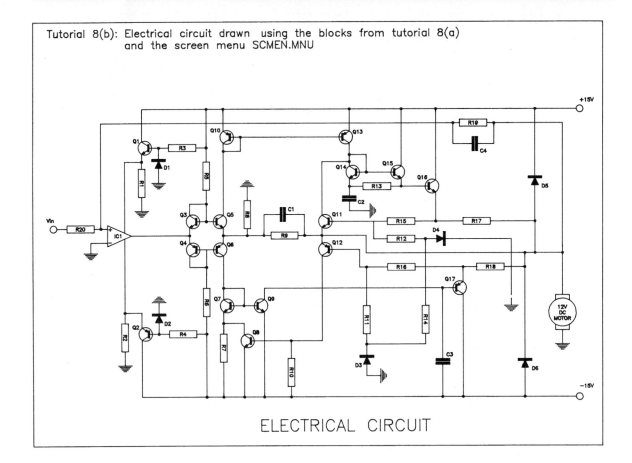

ELECTRICAL CIRCUIT

Index